A Case of Daylight Robbery

What My Church Did Not Teach Me

By
Peter Spreckley

Copyright © 2023 Peter Spreckley
First published in 2023

The right of Peter Spreckley to be identified as the author of this work has been asserted by him in accordance with the Copyright, Designs and Patents Act 1988.

All rights reserved. No part of this publication may be reproduced, stored in a retrieval system, or transmitted in any other form or by any means, electronic, mechanical, photocopying, recording or otherwise, without the prior permission of the publisher.

Unless otherwise marked, Scripture quotations are taken from the *Holy Bible*, New King James Version®. Copyright © 1982 by Thomas Nelson.
Used by permission.
All rights reserved.

Scripture quotations marked NLT are taken from the *Holy Bible*, New Living Translation. Copyright © 1996, 2004, 2015 by Tyndale House Foundation. Used by permission of Tyndale House Publishers, Inc., Carol Stream, Illinois 60188, USA. All rights reserved.

Published by Pearmont Publishing

Back story

This is an unusual book because the author, a retired solicitor, has little theological training, yet he is writing it as one who has heard from the Lord and has been commissioned to share what He wants His wider church to proclaim to the world, foundational truths of the Gospel of Jesus Christ where the church is failing to teach them. This is the back story.

In 1984 when Peter was a new-born babe in Christ, the first time he was prayed for he was told by the person praying that at some time in the future he would be walking across a plain saying "Thus saith the Lord." The word meant nothing to him at the time but in the spring of 2022, 38 years later, during which time he had not for one moment thought about the prophetic word, let alone contemplated writing a book., he found himself writing this book.

With the benefit of hindsight, it would seem the Lord was throughout those 38 years equipping him to write the book, which explores and reveals the significant truths his, Peter's, church, the Church of England, was not teaching him.

That was the several fundamental truths revealed in scripture which undergird the Gospel of Jesus Christ, which Peter has never heard preached in the nearly 70 years of attending Anglican churches. The fundamental truths reveal who we are in Christ and so our identity in Him.

In the book the reader may have his eyes opened to the headline scriptural truths which are not being taught, resulting in countless believers being robbed of the opportunity to find their identity in Christ. He may also, perhaps, see scriptures in a new context to the point of responding to them "Of course!"

How the New Covenant, which is a blood covenant, has made provision for the resources and assets of heaven to be available to born-again believers; what are the exceedingly great and precious promises in 2 Peter 1:4 which enable born-again believers to partake of the divine nature: the more than 21 changes which instantly occur when we are born again of the Holy Spirit: how faith is a spiritual force which requires corresponding action to be effective: how the verse "Man shall not live by bread alone, but by every word that proceeds from the mouth of God" is the "gold standard" for reading scripture.

Additionally, Peter looks at some teachings of Jesus which his church seems to have abandoned, such as the narrow and broad gates, hell, and the devil.

Peter's story is of a lukewarm churchgoer set on fire by the Holy Spirit and so equipped to serve the Master in the works prepared beforehand for him to do.

If the reader questions the involvement of God behind the contents of the book, confirmation can be found in chapter 27, which recounts the spectacular physical miracle Peter experienced when he threatened to scrap the book.

Table of Contents

Foreword .... *vii*
Introduction .... *ix*

1. How it Started 1
2. Before Christ 3
3. What Happened Next 5
4. The New Covenant - Part 1 and Part 2 13
5. The Eyes of Faith 21
6. Faith 27
7. Exceedingly Great and Precious Promises 33
8. The Promises – Believing and Receiving 37
9. What We Receive on Our New Birth 41
10. The Word of God 49
11. Why Should I Believe Every Word that Proceeds from the Mouth of God? 55
12. Why I Must Be Born Again 59
13. The Level Playing Field 65
14. Travellers' Joy 67
15. The Will of God – Finding It 71
16. Knowing God 75
17. The Kingdom of Heaven 79
18. The Full Gospel Business Men's Fellowship International (FGB) 83
19. The Power of God 91
20. The Baptism in the Holy Spirit 97
21. The Name of Jesus 101
22. Healing 105
23. The Narrow Gate and The Broad Gate 109

24. Hell	115
25. The Devil	119
26. "The Conclusion of the Whole Matter"	123
27. Postscript: Facing the Challenge	129
Acknowledgements	*133*

Foreword by Cannon Andrew White (Vicar of Baghdad)

I have read and written many books in my life. I honestly do not think I have ever been as challenged by any book as I have been by this one. Admittedly it is written by my father-in-law, Peter Spreckley, who I very much love and respect.

He was a much-respected lawyer and lay Christian leader, but what he has done here is to go through the fundamental teachings of the church, showing how they are fundamentally denying the true reality of the God who was made flesh and came and dwelt amongst us. Jesus was fired by the ever-living fire and power of the Holy Spirit, for He is indeed the One Who is and was and is the One to come.

Peter has rightly directed such thoughts towards the Church of England for he grew up in that national church. The fact is, though, that the challenges raised in the book could equally apply to most protestant churches throughout the world, whether Anglican, Lutheran or Methodist.

The one good thing is that amongst many of these churches there has been a major change in their popular theology, whilst liturgically they still might not think they are worthy to pick up the crumbs under the table. However, when the Holy Spirit becomes central to their worshipping community they are set on fire for the King of kings. Peter's life experience has been that fire, which has taken him from lukewarm churchgoer to "complete in Him" (Colossians 2:10).

What this book teaches us is that church which is not set on fire by the Holy Spirit is nothing more than boring church that so many people feel they need to escape from. The good news is that when church is infused with the Spirit of the Living G-d it becomes a fire house.

Peter has shown that the reality is that we are facing a major challenge, which is how can we ensure that the challenge of the church is relevant and now? It must not and cannot be daylight robbery in essence.

The gift of God's kingdom is a gift of life in all its fullness. That is what has been stolen by church bureaucracy. This book challenges the very nature of that terrible crime. What should we, the masses, do in response? The questions that Peter poses here are indeed part of this response.

CANON DR ANDREW P.B. WHITE, DD, PhD

Introduction

> "The hour is coming, and now is, when the true worshippers will worship the Father in spirit and truth; for the Father is seeking such to worship Him" (John 4:23).

This book, which, as I explain later, God has led me to write, is about how I was dead and how I came alive; was blind and how I came to see. How I, as a supposedly faithful member of my church, found excitement, adventure and transformation of my life, the possibility for which had been hidden from me for forty years.

How mining the scriptures opened a treasure-trove of riches and led to a transformed relationship with my heavenly Father and His Son Jesus Christ, as well as changing nearly every part of my life, which treasure-trove God made available 2,000 years ago for whoever believes. Specifically, it is about how I came to discover who I truly am in Christ, which turned out to be totally different from what my church had been teaching me.

By "my church" I refer only to the Church of England ("the church") which I have attended for some seventy years and in which I was christened as an infant in the church pictured on the cover (or so my mother later told me) and confirmed at the age of fifteen at Marlborough College. Neither my parents nor my three godparents had any faith that I was aware of.

It is about how I stumbled on the *"exceedingly great and precious promises"* in 2 Peter 1:4. I had never heard of these promises, and I have never heard since any teaching or discussion about them.

Yet in these verses is clearly stated that the purpose of the promises is to enable us to be *"partakers of the divine nature"* and in the promises is revealed how God has already done that amazing transformation in us, for us to become partakers of the divine nature through our knowledge of Him, by faith. In these verses is revealed God's purpose for my life and the lives of all mankind.

I am a *"whoever"* and this is my story. I write it to share it with anyone who, like I did, dares to believe there has to be more to being a Christian than they are experiencing or, indeed, anyone who is searching for the truth and is interested in knowing what God the Father, through His Son Jesus Christ, has already planned and provided for him or her – if only.

At the beginning of 2022 the thought of writing a book had never crossed my mind. I was then, as I had been for the previous thirty-nine years since I came to faith in 1984, pursuing God. I have never put limits on God, and I never doubted that He had more for me, which was and is the stimulus to always wanting to know Him better.

It was only during the latter years that I began to be aware of the gulf between the teaching I had been receiving within the church over the seventy years, and the teaching which was based on the word of God as revealed in scripture, which I was receiving from ministries and teachers from outside the church (see the Acknowledgements for details of the major ministries which have influenced my journey of discovery).

This teaching I have sought and followed from my new birth in 1984, when I came to a true faith, when I was born again and

Introduction

later baptised as a believer in our swimming pool. The gulf was, as I say, between what the church had been teaching me as to "who I am in Christ" and what scripture teaches me.

This is what this book is all about, because I reluctantly have to say that over time I have come to the conviction that I was, together with countless others, being robbed of the opportunity of finding out who we, as born-again believers, are in Christ and, as a consequence, were being robbed of the life in all its fullness promised by Him to His followers; in other words, our inheritance as revealed in scripture.

My story is how I discovered the riches of that inheritance and have by the grace of God – because I certainly did not deserve it – enjoyed a fuller, transformed and blessed life, which has been more than I could have ever asked for or imagined.

To say that I have been robbed is a challenge to the church, and to me if I have got it wrong and the challenge is not justified. The reader will come to his or her own view after reading this book, or by his or her own study of the scriptures.

In my own journey of discovery, I have found that there are so many fundamental truths revealed in scripture which have never, in my long experience in the church, been taught, so, by default, rendering me ineffectual as a witness to the gospel.

For instance, I now know, and scripture will confirm, that on my new birth I received the same faith and Holy Spirit power that the apostles received at Pentecost, to equip me, not just me but every born-again believer, to play our part, albeit imperfectly, in the "great commission" envisaged in Matthew 28:18-20, thereby producing *"fruit that should last"* (John 15:5).

With no teaching a baby remains a baby, and if I had not looked outside the church for spiritual food, I too would have remained a spiritual baby.

"As newborn babes, desire the sincere milk of the word, that you may grow thereby" (1 Peter 2:2).

In the following chapters I explore and share the principal foundational truths which were denied me, including during my training to be a lay reader, until I came to an understanding of them, which has enabled me to grow spiritually to the point where I have been equipped to write this book.

It was only after I had been writing for two months that, in the middle of one night, I was reminded that shortly after my new birth and baptism in the Holy Spirit in December 1984, when I attended my first dinner with the Full Gospel Business Men's Fellowship International (FGB)[1] in the Holiday Inn in Portsmouth, something unexpected happened. Professor Roy Peacock was the speaker. After the appeal for those seeking salvation (when yet again I surrendered my life to Jesus), I went forward for prayer. As Roy Peacock was praying for me, he said, and these are the exact words he used, "I see you walking across a plain saying, 'Thus saith the Lord.'"

As a babe in Christ those words meant nothing to me at that time, and it is only now, with the benefit of hindsight, that I believe the Lord was talking about this book – thirty-nine years ahead! If I am right about that I find it an encouraging confirmation.

---

[1] In 2011 the Full Gospel Business Men's Fellowship International divided and the UK Fellowship became the Full Gospel Business Men's Fellowship UK & Ireland which I continue to refer to as "FGB".

Introduction

"For though by this time you ought to be teachers, you need someone to teach you again the first principles of the oracles of God; and you have come to need milk and not solid food. For everyone who partakes only of milk is unskilled in the word of righteousness, for he is a babe. But solid food belongs to those who are of full age, that is, those who by reason of use have their senses exercised to discern both good and evil" (Hebrews 5:12-14).

In conversation with Christian friends, I had started to share how I was learning what the church had not taught me, but I had no intention of recording it until one day in February, when I was visiting my friend the Reverend Tony Roake (under whom I had served as a lay reader). He seemed to burst out, "You must write it down." When I resisted, he said, in terms, that if just one person came to faith because of reading it, it would be worth it. Something inside me seemed to agree, and so the idea for this book was born in me.

Up to 1984 my background, as described later, would have classified me, I suspect, as a traditional churchgoer, even a pillar of the church. It was surely assumed by the church and by me that I was a Christian because of my having been christened as a baby and confirmed, and I went to church.

But, as I was in 1984 to learn, I was not a Christian because I had never confessed Jesus as my Lord, nor had I believed in my heart that God had raised Him from the dead, so I was not saved, and Jesus was at that stage neither my Lord nor my Saviour (Romans 10:10). This explains why what I was saying in church had no hold on me and I was able to live a lifestyle which contradicted my empty words spoken by rote.

I admit that I am writing as someone who has effectively had no academic training in theology, but scripture, the word of God, has been given to us with the Holy Spirit to teach us when we search for the truth (see chapter 13).

My story relates exclusively to my personal experiences in the church and outside, and the revelation (I use the term advisedly) which I came into through the grace of God, through deep study of His word with the Holy Spirit as my teacher, as well as from the ministries I have mentioned, leading me to an ever-deepening knowledge of who I truly am in Christ. In the book I have identified foundational truths which are there in scripture for every genuine seeker after the truth.

I have sought to share them in a light and non-exhaustive, perhaps simplistic but practical way, which seems relevant to our daily walk with God. Each of the foundational truths warrants deeper teaching and study, which is, if not being taught in our churches, available online or through other media.

An alternative title for this book could equally be *What Happens When You Believe the Word of God*. This is because, from the start, I determined, consciously or unconsciously, to believe the Bible without challenge. The teaching which I have subsequently received has been from ministries and teachers which/who base their teaching without compromise on belief in the inerrant truth of the Bible.

In short, the gulf between what the church was and is teaching, which is, as I understand it based on what the order of services require me to confess, that I am a sinner saved by Jesus' sacrifice on the cross through which I have the expectation of eternal life, and in the meanwhile I remain unworthy to pick up the crumbs from under His table and I remain dependent on His mercy.

I utterly embrace and thank God for Jesus' substitutionary death. I was indeed a sinner but only until I received mercy

Introduction

through Jesus' death on the cross, when on my new spiritual birth God made me not only a new creation in Christ but also the righteousness of God in Him and I received eternal life there and then.

I was made at the same time a son of God and a member of His family. Jesus became my spiritual brother, I became a partaker in the divine nature, and I am already a citizen of the kingdom of heaven (see chapter 9). That is some gulf!

Yes, I do still sin, of course I do, but if I confess my sin, Jesus is *"faithful and just to forgive us our sins and to cleanse us from all unrighteousness"* (1 John 1:9). If cleansed from all unrighteousness, then I become again righteous in the eyes of God. That is why we must keep short accounts with God.

The implications for the church, which is the body of Christ, are truly serious. Ignorance of our inheritance will rob the church's members of what is rightfully ours, and ignorance of the fundamental truth of the absolute need to be born again as the condition precedent to entry to the kingdom of heaven may rob us of our salvation if following the church's teaching leads us to sleepwalk into an unthinkable eternity.

To confirm this, I draw the reader's attention to a scripture which has grown in significance as I have been writing this book.

"Enter by the narrow gate; for wide is the gate and broad is the way that leads to destruction, and there are many who go in by it. Because narrow is the gate and difficult is the way which leads to life, and there are few who find it" (Matthew 7:13-14).

The Church of England seems to take pride in being a "broad church". I cannot help feeling that by the grace of God I may have had a narrow escape! (See chapter 23.)

I underline that this is my story of seventy years as a member of the Church of England under, since our marriage in 1962, at least fifteen vicars.

I also need to make clear that I have heard of or attended Church of England churches where the Holy Spirit is manifestly present and moving. I am sure that many believers will read what I have written and be able to say, "Yes, I know and have experienced that." I certainly hope so. Others will have their own stories of how God has moved in their lives, and I thank Him for that.

On the other hand, any lack of teaching, that is lack of discipling, on the fundamental truths which I have been led to highlight, will have resulted in countless numbers of those attending their church, by default, being robbed of, if not their salvation, their full inheritance through the new covenant (see chapter 4).

I trust that it will become clear from my story, as well as from the relevant scriptures, that however undeserving we are, and we all are, we may find transformation from what we may have resigned ourselves to being for the rest of our lives, to be recipients of a new, eternal and abundant life here and now on this earth, not only for ourselves but also making a difference for others, which is what we are each called to do.

"Go therefore and make disciples of all nations, baptising them in the name of the Father and of the Son and of the Holy Spirit, teaching them to observe all things that I have commanded you; and lo, I am with you always, even to the end of the age" (Mathew 28:19-20).

I am aware that every time I suggest that the Lord has been instrumental in my writing this book, some may, understand-

Introduction

ably, wonder whether I might be deceiving myself into making this claim.

But wonderfully and supernaturally the Lord has surely confirmed that this is His book, not only by the prophetic word I have mentioned but also by the extraordinary miracle of healing He worked in me when I was, as the result of circumstances which had arisen, considering that I would have to scrap the book altogether. I have recounted the full story of this in chapter 27.

Scriptures quoted are from the New King James Version except where marked NLT which are from The New Living Translation.

CHAPTER 1

How it Started

It all started one day in the summer of 1984 when a strange thing happened to me. As I often did, I was mowing the grass in the churchyard adjoining our house in West Sussex. I loved doing it because it made me feel "good". The "strange" thing about this event was that I suddenly stopped mowing and found myself saying to myself, "I wonder if God is *real*. I don't know what all this is about." It was also "strange" because I had been attending that church for fourteen years, and before that, from the age of eight onwards, I had been attending chapels and churches wherever I was living at the time.

I had been christened as a baby and confirmed at the age of fifteen. My parents were, as far as I was aware, atheists (we never ever talked about faith, or church, and when the vicar came it was for a glass of sherry).

Having had the thought and asked the question in the churchyard, I wondered who I could talk to about it. But I could not think of anyone, and that included vicars, who had talked about experiencing the reality of God. If ever they had done so, I certainly missed it.

Without a better idea, I decided to go to the public library, which was next to my office in Petersfield, where I "looked up" God in the religious books section. So started an amazing adventure with Him which continues today, starting with a transformation of my relationship with the Father, His Son Jesus Christ, and the Holy Spirit. I now know that such is not unique to me, but can be the experience of every believer, no two stories ever being the same. What followed I continue in chapter 3.

At this point I need to stress again that my church attendances were almost exclusively in Anglican churches, and, secondly, that I am only talking about my personal experience of, as opposed to just belief in, scripture.

We are each unique and our relationship with God is just that, but we do all share the same manual, the word of God, as revealed in scripture, so we should each be on the same journey in our own way but to the same destination, the specific directions to which have been clearly signed in that same word.

I am going to divide my life story into three parts: before Christ (BC), and after I had encountered Him, with a short explanation in between of how it happened.

CHAPTER 2

Before Christ

"And you He made alive, who were dead in trespasses and sin" (Ephesians 2:1).

It is difficult to be wholly objective and so truly honest about my life before my encounter with God. One word immediately springs to mind – hypocrite! If saying one thing in church on a Sunday but doing the opposite during the following week qualified me for that, then that is what I was – on stilts!

The qualification for that sobriquet was that my professions of faith in church had no conviction, which meant they had no hold on my life, so I was able to justify to myself behaviour which would have disqualified me from both the kingdom of heaven and the matrimonial home.

Yes, I would have said I believed in God and Jesus, and His death on the cross, but in truth no more than I believed in Wellington and his victory at Waterloo. What took me to church was, I would say, the feel-good factor or, perhaps, that my doing so was pleasing to God and might be to my credit at some time in the future.

I was not oblivious to God, and there were periods, I would call them religious periods, in my early life when I had felt drawn to Him, whoever He was, but it was more an instinct than a need for salvation. You might say that I had a heart for God.

At Cambridge University I even had thoughts of being ordained. Yet at the same time, while attending occasional evensongs in chapel, I was laughing at the committed Christians who met mid-week to pray.

Looking back on these moments I am reminded of the saying of Jesus, "*No one can come to Me unless the Father who sent Me draws him*" (John 6:44). They now seem to me to have been, perhaps, part of God's drawing me to Jesus.

If I had been taught just a fraction of what I have subsequently learned, things might have been very different. In the event, God, working through and with the help of my dear wife Mary, was gracious enough to restore our marriage.

I went back to churchgoing and helping as before, where my spiritual ignorance or lack of faith, which was never questioned or challenged, was not a barrier to my being voted onto the PCC and, later, elected to be a churchwarden. I would have expected that to have been my "faith" story for the rest of my life, but God had other plans.

CHAPTER 3

What Happened Next

"And you will seek Me, and find Me, when you search for Me with all your heart" (Jeremiah 29:13).

In the library, as I have recorded, I started in the religious books section intending to "look up" God. Being Anglican I started with hardbacks, including reading about St Augustine who certainly encountered the reality of God, but I did not find in those books a convincing answer there to my question about the reality of God as a personal experience, until I picked out some paperbacks.

At this stage the Holy Spirit began to speak to me. These books, written by men and women still alive or recently dead, talked about a living relationship with Jesus and through Him the Father.

They testified to Christians experiencing transformed lives, healings, and miracles. It seemed that their lives were akin to what the first disciples must have experienced in the early years of the church after Pentecost. Helpfully, they referred to the Bible references which confirmed that what was happening was authenticated by scripture.

I had absolutely no idea that God-related experiences could happen, but I was so excited by what I was reading that from that moment on I wanted to experience the same relationship and experiences.

So, I started passionately to pursue God for everything He had for me, and I still do! But first I had to learn that despite more than thirty-five years of attending churches, I was nowhere near being a Christian. Why? Because I had not been born again (see chapter 12), which I had at an early stage, through the teaching in those books, learned is a prior condition to becoming a Christian.

I had no idea what being born again meant until it was explained in the books. But when I understood what being born again actually involved, I wanted it so badly that I got on my knees at home one night and, after seeking forgiveness for my many sins, I confessed Jesus as my Lord, and I invited Him into my heart as Lord and Saviour.

I had found a Bible, one of several which had remained unread on the bookshelf for years, and I began to look up the Bible references given in the paperbacks, and then started reading chunks of the New Testament. Strangely, what before had seemed so irrelevant now started to become understandable, even obvious.

The more I read, the more I wanted to read, and the more the words started to feed my hunger for more. All this happened without any human involvement.

What was most important at this stage was that I had an open mind, by which I mean that I had put out of my mind my thirty-five-year church experience, which was, for me, not difficult because of the total lack of impact on me from attending church. So, there were no barriers, such as doctrines or traditions, to my hungry reading of the word, acting on it and then experiencing it.

In December 1984 (when, by the way, I was a churchwarden), I was invited by a friend to attend a rally in the Guildhall

What Happened Next

in Portsmouth, put on by the group called the Full Gospel Business Men's Fellowship International (FGB),[2] about which Fellowship I share in chapter 18. That evening the speaker was one Isabel Chapman, who had ministered in the Far East.

When she had finished her testimony, she invited people who wanted to commit their lives to Jesus to raise their hand. Although I had already made my commitment to Him, and so had an excuse for not responding and so avoiding what before might have been embarrassing for an Anglican churchgoer, my arm literally raised itself.

Then, when invited for prayer, I rushed forward, again something which before I would have been reluctant to do in public. Remember I was a dyed-in-the-wool Anglican, and British!

While Isabel Chapman prayed for those of us who had gone forward, I experienced the power of the Holy Spirit on me as I stood there, and I started to shake. Others were falling under the power of the Holy Spirit, and, in my naivety, I wanted to call an ambulance!

This was my first experience of the manifested power of God. He was already answering the question I asked when I was in the churchyard. This was real.

I ordered a tape recording of the meeting, and when it arrived, I played it to my wife Mary (who had not been at the meeting) as we were going to bed. When the recording reached the point where the power of God had fallen on me at the meeting, the Holy Spirit fell on me again.

But this time not just on me, but in me and, as it were, pumping through me, for about half an hour. I have described

---

[2] See note to the Introduction.

it as experiencing something like an electric current but without the shock.

Afterwards I had difficulty in standing up, and if anyone had seen me, they would have said I was drunk – and so I was, but not on wine but on the Holy Spirit (Acts 2:15).

I got up transformed in so many ways: for instance, in our marriage and family, in my attitude to my work, the end of a drink problem and my attitude to life generally.

However, this book is not about me as a human being but whom I am in Christ, and how I discovered the answer to that through the foundational truths which I have since 1984 come to understand.

These truths had been there in scripture all the time, but in all my years of churchgoing I had never heard of them, let alone any teaching on them. I am convinced that my recollection of the lack of teaching before 1984 is accurate because since then I have been very alert to what was being preached and nothing has changed, at least not when I have been in the congregation. Thus, the discovery of the *"exceedingly great and precious promises"* (2 Peter 1:4) which God has made available to us was something totally new to me, as were the foundational truths which I will unpack.

This is just the background to my journey which was to lead me to understand the wonder of who I am in Christ.

This was not a lightbulb moment – the journey continues today – but over the thirty-nine years since I started on it, I have, by the grace of God, been privileged to come into a deeper understanding of God's equipping of His followers, which is revealed in the gospels and epistles, and which, in short, is that we should in every way – yes, every way – be like Jesus and doing the same things He did, and even greater things (John 14:12)!

Peter tells us clearly that God's plan for each of us is that we should be *"partakers of the divine nature"* (2 Peter 1:4), that is, just like Jesus!

Understanding the promises is to understand how God has opened the way for that to happen in every believer's life. I have often heard talk of trying to be like Jesus, but this was by our own efforts, that is imitating Jesus.

But scripture teaches us that all the believer needs to do is to understand the promises, believe them and receive them by faith. They are God's free gift to us through the blood covenant (see chapter 4), and that includes partaking in the divine nature (see chapter 9).

This should not come as a surprise because scripture makes it clear that at the end Jesus will present the church to Himself, *"a glorious church, not having spot or wrinkle or any such thing, but that she should be holy and without blemish"* (Ephesians 5:27). That's us, so no wonder we mere mortals, with all our imperfections, need to become partakers of the divine nature if we are to be included.

That is what Paul was endeavouring to achieve as he explains in Colossians 1:28, *"Him we preach, warning every man and teaching every man in all wisdom, that we may present every man perfect in Christ Jesus."*

I would liken the process of discovery to doing a jigsaw puzzle. Piece by piece one builds the picture until the whole is revealed.

In our house, when we started a jigsaw puzzle we always began by getting the outside pieces out first and completing the outside before beginning on the picture itself. In this case, having the outside in place first is imperative because the outside of this picture is the everlasting and unconditional love of God. Without that there would be no picture.

Within it I find a picture which reflects the superlatives that describe the working out of God's love in and through Jesus, for instance, *"the manifold wisdom of God"* (Ephesians 3:10), *"the unsearchable riches of Christ"* (Ephesians 3:8), *"the exceedingly great and precious promises"* (2 Peter 1:4), *"in whom are hidden all the treasures of wisdom and knowledge"* (Colossians 2:3) and *"what are the riches of the glory of this mystery among the Gentiles: which is Christ in you, the hope of glory"* (Colossians 1:27).

In the following pages I will endeavour to put the pieces of the jigsaw puzzle together. As I have said, I am not an academic nor a theologian but, as I share later, there is encouraging news for those of us in a similar position: *"God has chosen the foolish things of the world to put to shame the wise"* (1 Corinthians 1:27).

So that we "whoevers" can each come to a place where we can sing with John Newton, "I once was lost but now am found, was blind but now I see." I share my story in the hope that others who may, without realising it, be blind, as I was, have their spiritual eyes opened to see what riches God has, through Jesus and the blood covenant given us, and for which we do not have to strive.

Although I had some limited training when later I was licensed as a lay reader in July 1997, my story is just my personal story, but shows how anyone who seeks God unconditionally with all his or her heart, believing the Bible to be inerrant truth, as best he or she is able, can find his or her own story. I treasure those words "as best he can" because we can feel guilty that we are not meeting the target of 100 per cent which God seems to demand, but, of course, He does not, only "the very best we can".

In the following chapters I deal with how my journey over the last thirty-nine years has taken me to a fuller understanding of who I truly am in Christ. But please remember who I was before 1984, to get a picture of the wonder of God's grace.

My basic qualification is that I was and am the person Jesus, who has no favourites, was so often addressing as "whoevers". That is the starting point for every seeker, as Jesus points out in John 3:16, *"God so loved the world that He gave His only begotten Son, that **whoever** believes in Him should not perish but have everlasting life."*

When I started my journey of discovery, I had no idea that what I was to learn from the scriptures, as they gradually revealed their secrets, was to challenge much of what I had learned or picked up from teaching in the churches I attended about my understanding of God and my relationship with Him – which at the start in 1984 was almost zero. Hence my questioning God as I was mowing the grass in the churchyard, "Is He real and what's it all about?"

CHAPTER 4

The New Covenant - Part 1 and Part 2

"This is My blood of the new covenant, which is shed for many for the remission of sins" (Matthew 26:28).

Over the years, as I grew in my knowledge and understanding of God, I learned many new (to me) truths. Many of them related to who I am in Christ, which I only came to more fully understand when I came upon a book by E.W. Kenyon titled *The Blood Covenant: The Hidden Truth Revealed at the Lord's Table*,[3] which I recommend to anyone seeking to understand how God's new plan for the salvation of mankind was initiated and sealed.

Of course, I, along with everyone else partaking in a Church of England communion service, was familiar with the reference to *"This is My blood of the new covenant, which is shed for many for the remission of sins."* But I never questioned what the terms of the covenant were until I read Kenyon's book. Before that I assumed that the covenant was Jesus dying in my place to pay the price for my sin so that I did not have to, thus qualifying me for heaven.

When I read the book for the first time, I was taken totally by surprise by what it was about, and how it was and is the key to a person understanding who he or she is in Christ, and who

---

[3] E.W. Kenyon, *The Blood Covenant: The Hidden truth Revealed at the Lord's Table* (Whitaker House, 2020).

we are in the body of Christ. Kenyon reveals the working out of God's plan for those of us who are in Christ, to grow us into what He has prepared for us to be, as revealed in scripture.

By this I mean our calling to be *"like Jesus here in this world"* (1 John 4:17 NLT), being *"complete in Him"* (Colossians 2:10) and *"be mature in the Lord, measuring up to the full and complete standard of Christ"* (Ephesians 4:13 NLT). And, again, *"partakers of the divine nature"*, all of this being the destiny for us here on earth as soon as we are born again of the Holy Spirit.

In short, the terms of the blood covenant are such that we are enabled to be just like Jesus, if we only understand and so can receive what God has already done for us to qualify us for the kingdom of heaven, from the moment of our new birth.

No wonder then that we read in Hebrews 8:6, *"But now He has obtained a more excellent ministry, in as much He is also Mediator of a better covenant, which was established on better promises."*

Jesus said at the last supper, *"This is My blood of the new covenant"* (Matthew 26:28), so the New Covenant was a "blood" covenant. I had never heard any teaching on the new covenant let alone a "blood" covenant.

I will therefore, when referring to the new covenant, call it "the blood covenant" to underline the cost to Jesus who entered into it on our behalf, and its provision for us to have access to all the resources of heaven, which through the exceedingly great and precious promises enables us to be partakers of the divine nature.

I learned through E.W. Kenyon's book that a blood covenant is the oldest known and strongest covenant in human history. It was primarily used where a strong tribe lived beside a weaker tribe and the latter was in fear of being destroyed. The weaker tribe would seek to "cut" a covenant with the stronger tribe to have the stronger tribe's protection.

The common process was for the leader of each party to take a cup of wine and for each of them to make an incision in his own arm, so the blood drips into the same cup. The wine is stirred, then the two parties drink the wine.

The covenant was regarded as sacred and there were fearful consequences if one party broke it. Deadly enemies would become trusted friends when they had cut a covenant. The moment a blood covenant is solemnised everything that a blood covenant party owns in the world is at the disposal of his blood brother, the other party, if he needs it.

This is well demonstrated by the recorded results of the blood covenants cut by David Livingstone and Henry Stanley with the leaders of the tribes they were seeking to teach about Jesus.

The wonderful thing is that because the moment we surrender our life to Jesus as Lord and Saviour, we are instantly born again of the Holy Spirit from above. At that moment we are in Christ, and He is in us, so that in Him we become inheritors of the benefits of the blood covenant between God the Father and Jesus and sealed by Jesus' blood.

Thereby all the resources of heaven – including the divine nature, divine gifts, divine promises, divine love, divine health, grace, mercy, wisdom, faith, power and more – become available to us when we need them. That is grace! The working out of this in our lives is explained in 2 Peter 1:2-4:

"Grace and peace be multiplied to you in the knowledge of God and of Jesus our Lord, as His divine power has given to us all

things that pertain to life and godliness, through the knowledge of Him who called us by glory and virtue, by which have been given to us exceedingly great and precious promises, that through these you may be partakers of the divine nature, having escaped the corruption that is in the world through lust."

In those few words, *"His divine power has given to us all things that pertain to life and godliness,"* is revealed what becomes available to us by virtue of the blood covenant as God's gift when we come into a saving knowledge of Him, to be received by us by faith, which we can only exercise when we know what is that gift.

When my spiritual eyes were opened to these verses and the vital truths revealed in them, I found they unlocked so many scriptures which show me who I am as a new creation, a recipient of promises which before would have been beyond my wildest dreams.

It is difficult for the human mind to take in the wonder of this truth where we, having been born again, have available to us through the blood covenant all the resources of heaven. Jesus foretold the coming of the kingdom.

"Therefore do not worry, saying, 'What shall we eat?' or 'What shall we drink?' or 'What shall we wear?' For after all these things the Gentiles seek. For your heavenly Father knows you need all these things. But seek first the kingdom of God and His righteousness, and all these things shall be added to you" (Matthew 6:31-33).

Jesus was looking ahead to the blood covenant, through which God would take over the supply chain to provide for the needs of His family. J

Jesus was effectively saying, "The time will come, when you have been born again, that is transferred from the kingdom of darkness into the kingdom of heaven (Colossians 1:13) and become the righteousness of God in Christ (2 Corinthians 5:21) then you will have access to the resources of heaven for all your needs."

Now I understand how we can declare, *"I can do all things through Christ who strengthens me"* (Philippians 4:13) and *"My God shall supply all your need according to His riches in glory by Christ Jesus"* (Philippians 4:19).

If we understand that the resources of heaven are now available to us when received by faith, then scriptures such as the two just quoted sit comfortably into the terms of the blood covenant, and we can say in response to them, "Of course!"

It follows from this understanding of what the blood covenant has made available to, and has already been fulfilled for, every believer that we must cease asking God to, in terms, "do it again" – that is, asking Him to do again what He has already done.

On the cross Jesus, *"knowing that all things were now accomplished,"* said, *"It is finished!"* (John 19:28-30) indicating that His mission was completed, the covenant was fulfilled. So, rather than asking Him for our physical and spiritual needs, for instance for more power, more mercy, more wisdom, or greater strength, we should be thanking Him for having provided already for whatever we need at the time and meditate on it, claim it by faith and walk in it.

What I have shared about the wonder of the new covenant is little more than an introduction, and perhaps has whet the appetite of the reader to know more of the wonder of *"the treasures of wisdom and knowledge"* hidden in Christ (Colossians 2:3).

Part 2: The Bigger Picture

The blood covenant and what it releases to the born-again believer has to be seen in the context of the bigger picture, by which I mean the creation story recounted in the first three chapters of the Bible where we find the story of the greatest (daylight) robbery which was ever to take place.

The last step of God's creation was His making Adam, and later Eve, in His own image with the declared purpose for them of having *"dominion over... all the earth and over every creeping thing that creeps on the earth"* (Genesis 1:26).

The first thing He did after creating Adam and Eve was to bless them with the instruction, *"Be fruitful and multiply; fill the earth and subdue it; have dominion over the fish of the sea, over the birds of the air, and over every living thing that moves on the earth"* (1:28).

God put Adam in the Garden of Eden to tend and keep it, saying, *"Of every tree of the garden you may freely eat; but of the tree of the knowledge of good and evil you shall not eat, for in the day you eat from it you shall surely die"* (2:15-17).

If we believe that Adam was created in the image of God, we can from our revealed knowledge of God impute to him some inherited God-like characteristics. For instance, he was a partaker of the divine nature, he was complete in God, and he had the fullness of God in him.

He was free from sin and sickness, he had an intimate spiritual relationship with God who is spirit, he had authority/dominion over all the earth and everything that moved on it, including the serpent. He did not suffer fear and anxiety. In short, he was not troubled by any of the many trials and tribulations which mankind has experienced ever since, we all being inheritors of Adam's sin nature.

But then the great robbery! The serpent who/which we now know was the devil of whom Jesus said, *"He was a murderer from the beginning, and does not stand in the truth, because there is no truth in him. When he speaks a lie, he speaks from his own resources, for he is a liar and the father of it"* (John 8:44).

Within a short exchange he had persuaded Eve, who in turn persuaded Adam, who originally had received the instruction, *"Of the tree of the knowledge of good and evil you shall not eat,"* to eat of the fruit of the tree, thereby preferring the devil's word to God's, and consequently they suffered the sentence God had forewarned of.

Adam died not physically but spiritually and so forfeited his spiritual identity with God and caused himself, and through him all mankind, to be separated from God by our sin. At the same time, he forfeited his authority and dominion over the earth to the devil, which is the explanation for the statement in 1 John 5:19, *"We know that we are of God, and the whole world lies under the sway of the wicked one."*

Coming back to the blood covenant, through which Jesus made the way for our new birth from above, we become recipients by faith of the exceedingly great and precious promises through which we become partakers of the divine nature (2 Peter 1:4), just as Adam was when he was created. This will, I trust, become clear in the following chapters.

Suffice to say at this stage that through the covenanted promises, Jesus on the cross achieved the restoration to us of everything that had been lost when Adam and Eve, through their disobedience to the word of God, died spiritually. This will be dealt with in chapter 9 in which I identify our inheritance from our new birth.

This foundational truth reveals the power and authority which has been available to the church, yet over the centuries has been ignored, or simply misunderstood. It is not hard to imagine the effect that ignorance has had on the witness of the church during that time. If only . . . !

CHAPTER 5

The Eyes of Faith

"But the natural man does not receive the things of the Spirit of God, for they are foolishness to him" (1 Corinthians 2:14).

One of the first things I had to learn if I was to deepen my relationship with the Lord was that there are two levels of seeing and two levels of believing.

This might come as a surprise to many. It certainly was new to me after my original encounter with the Lord in 1984. But I soon learned that the Bible contains spiritual as well as factual truths, and to understand spiritual truths requires seeing with spiritual eyes, which we are given when we are born again of the Holy Spirit.

"Most assuredly, I say to you, unless one is born again, he cannot see the kingdom of God" (John 3:3). How simple is that truth? When Jesus says "Most assuredly" or "Truly, truly" we really do have to pay close attention. No one had taught me about that fundamental truth, but when I was born again it was obvious! This scripture pops up again in chapters 9 and 12, "What we receive on our new birth" and "Why we must be born again."

Paul prayed in his letter to the Ephesians that **"the eyes of your understanding being enlightened;** *that you may know what is the hope of His calling, what are the riches of the glory of His inheritance in the saints, and what is the exceeding great power toward us who believe"* (Ephesians 1:18-19).

Jesus said, *"It is the Spirit who gives life; the flesh profits nothing. The words that I speak to you are spirit, and they are life"* (John 6:63).

Without spiritual eyes one only uses one's natural senses, what we see, hear, taste, smell, and feel – often referred to in the Bible as "the flesh" – to try to understand truths which are spiritual.

Those without spiritual eyesight, by reason of the fact that they will be operating in the natural, will find some parts of scripture unbelievable. Once I started to read the scriptures through my spiritual eyes, my response became, "Of course."

Understanding this distinction is to understand how the scriptures, which promise so much, could be and are often read, or listened to, repeatedly without causing any response from the reader or hearer. It is as if we become immune to the words of God through repetition. Although the words read are in the spirit realm "spirit and life" They remain, if looked at through our senses, just lifeless words on a page (see also the 1 Corinthians 2:14 below). Seen through spiritual eyes they leap into eternal life.

There are three main scriptures which are key to the understanding of spiritual truths.

"However, we speak wisdom among those who are mature, yet not the wisdom of this age, nor of the rulers of this age, who are coming to nothing. But we speak the wisdom of God in a mystery, the hidden wisdom which God ordained before the ages for our glory" (1 Corinthians 2:6-7).

Continuing the same passage is the helpful explanation as to how spiritual understanding "works".

"Eye has not seen, nor ear heard, nor have entered into the heart of man the things which God has prepared for those who love him" (v. 9). That is through the natural senses.

I believe that for that reason most might understand and agree with that. But watch out! There is a "But" coming up. It has often been said that "But" in the Bible stands for "a blessed and undeniable truth coming" and this is, in the present case, just that.

*"**But** God has revealed them to us through His Spirit. For the Spirit searches all things, yes, the deep things of God. For what man knows the things of man except the spirit of man which is in him. Even so no one knows the things of God except the Spirit of God"* (v. 10-11).

"Now we have received, not the spirit of the world, but the Spirit who is from God, that we might know the things that have been freely given to us by God" (v. 12).

Under the blood covenant God has revealed what He has prepared for those who love Him. What that is can be found in the exceedingly great and precious promises so freely given. How it happens is explained below.

"These things we also speak, not in the words which man's wisdom teaches but which the Holy Spirit teaches, comparing spiritual things with spiritual" (v. 13).

"But the natural man does not receive the things of the Spirit of God, for they are foolish to him; nor can he know them, because they are spiritually discerned" (v. 14).

"But he who is spiritual judges all things, yet he himself is rightly judged by no one" (v. 15).

For me, the division between the two sources of information could not be more clearly explained. The passage tells us that we are only going to understand the spiritual truths of the Bible when we look with spiritual eyes. We are given these when we are born again and receive the Holy Spirit.

Finally, and almost triumphantly, Paul declares, *"'For who has known the mind of the Lord that he may instruct Him?' But we have the mind of Christ"* (v. 16). How? Through the Holy Spirit who *"knows the things of God"* dwelling within us.

The third scripture is found in Paul's letter to the Romans: *"Do not be conformed to this world, but be transformed by the renewing of your mind, that you may prove what is the good and acceptable and perfect will of God"* (Romans 12:2).

God is spirit and if we are to hear from Him, our communication must be direct through the Holy Spirit, or through His words, which are *"spirit and life"* (John 6:63 NLT). In instructing us to *"not be conformed to this world"* we may have to put aside our pre-conceived ideas or even, sometimes, our teaching or traditions of a lifetime.

In my case, this meant that I had to cancel my church mindset formed over the then thirty-five years of churchgoing, and be prepared, in common parlance, to look "outside the box". As I have mentioned, as soon as I did so my spiritual eyes began to be opened to what God was saying and doing outside my then understanding and experience. Then my adventure began.

It was only as I began, over time (it's been thirty-nine years so far), to become more familiar with the scriptures, that I came to understand more fully the spiritual truths which are there in the gospels and the epistles for anyone to see through eyes of faith, and so to understand who we truly are in Christ.

I started with a clean sheet in that, as already mentioned, I had discovered that after some thirty-five years of churchgoing I was not a Christian.

So, my mind was free from the influence of the church's teaching and traditions, which, subconsciously, I must have rejected, as evidenced by the very fact that in the graveyard conversation with God I was acknowledging that I had no idea whether He was real or what it was all about.

CHAPTER 6

Faith

> *"For whatever is born of God overcomes the world. And this is the victory that has overcome the world – our faith"* (1 John 5:4).

The source of our faith is Jesus who is the *"author and finisher of our faith"* (Hebrews 12:2). I understand that "finisher" can also be translated "developer."

Adam, when created by God, did not need faith because it was not necessary, he being in a perfect spiritual relationship with God.

If Jesus is the author and finisher/developer of our faith then we must be aware of our tendency to have faith in our own faith, which is a dead end because *"faith comes from hearing and hearing from the word of God"* (Romans 8:17). Furthermore, there is no limit on our faith other than a self-imposed one because Peter tells us we can have the same precious faith as he and the apostles had (2 Peter 1:1).

Over the years I have listened to teaching on faith on YouTube, I've read books and listened to CDs all about faith, by men who have deep understanding and experience of what it means to have the faith of God, not just faith in God; men with fruitful ministries, which are based on the two foundations of faith and love.

> *"For in Christ Jesus neither circumcision nor uncircumcision avails anything, but faith working through love"* (Galatians 5:6).

In all my years of attending church I don't recall any teaching on the subject. But as I have received teaching from such men, I have learned to grow in faith and walk more and more in it as I understand how it works.

I cannot overstate how relevant this is, because *"without faith it is impossible to please Him"* (Hebrews 11:6). Furthermore, without exercising faith and love we cannot benefit from God's provision for us under the blood covenant, because the promises are received by faith working through love.

I am acutely aware that my belief in the inerrancy of scripture and my understanding of how faith works is opening me to the charge that I have fallen for "positive confession" or "prosperity gospel" teaching, so often mocked by more traditional believers as "blab it and grab it" theology.

If it were just a question of individual belief, one can agree to differ. On the other hand, if the argument is about whether faith works, then those who have experienced the working of faith in circumstances where there is no room for a coincidence or natural cause explanation, have the advantage.

I have been privileged to have had an incontrovertible testimony of such an event.

Whilst personally I have in the past experienced healing in my body which I cannot prove, in chapter 27 I recount the serious health challenge with which I was faced in June 2022, and how I met the challenge by reliance on the word of God for my healing *"by whose stripes you were healed"* (1 Peter 2:24), which healing I received in a way which can only be described as so unnatural as to be miraculous and could only be the power of God at work, fulfilling 1 Peter 2:24.

The subject of faith is so essential for the believer, if only because of the Hebrews 11:6 scripture. If one studied faith for a lifetime, one would still be learning at the end. I only mention a few scriptures which have impacted my life and are relevant to the basic exercise of our faith. As explained below, there are laws of faith which we need to know if we are to operate within them and be fruitful.

Jesus Himself laid down the "ground rules" for seekers when He said, *"Assuredly, I say to you, whoever does not receive the kingdom of God as a little child will by no means enter it"* (Mark 10:15).

In other words, our attitude must be, in terms, "If my dad says it, I believe it." So, our faith must be in what God says, which is the word of God, meaning *"every word that proceeds from the mouth of the Lord"* (Deuteronomy 8:3).

This is where the conflict between reason and spiritual revelation kicks in. The battle is between faith and sense knowledge.

Faith calls for believing, as facts, things that do not exist or cannot be experienced by our five senses: sight, touch, hearing, taste and feeling. God Himself who *"gives life to the dead and calls those things which do not exist as though they did"* (Romans 4:17) exercised such faith when he created the heavens and the earth. He said, *"'Let there be light'; and there was light"* (Genesis 1:3).

This is in effect what we are required to do when we seek to exercise faith, that is "to call things which do not exist as though they do".

"Now faith is the substance of things hoped for, the evidence of things not seen" (Hebrews 11:1).

Sense knowledge is informed by the five senses. Our only weapon in this warfare is the word of God, which teaches us that there is a *"law of faith"* (Romans 3:27).

If there is a law of faith then there must be a right way and a wrong way of operating in it, but it is only when one begins to understand that there are laws that govern faith, and begin to learn what those laws are, that faith will begin to work, because faith is a spiritual force only when activated by our acting on it or speaking it.

"For assuredly, I say to you, whoever says to this mountain, 'Be removed and be cast into the sea,' and does not doubt in his heart, but believes that those things he says will be done, he will have whatever he says" (Mark 11:23).

The hard truth, which shook me at first, is that unless I am prepared to act on the relevant scripture, that scripture will do me no good, however much I believe it.

So, the subject of faith, where it comes from, how it operates, how it is activated by a corresponding action or word, *"faith without works is dead"* (James 2:17-20), and how, when activated, it is a spiritual force, is a profound subject, requiring deep study of the word.

In my case, I was greatly helped by the teaching of those who have spent a lifetime seeking the answers, and now experience daily the exceedingly great and precious promises covering every aspect of their lives. This includes signs and wonders as an integral part of their ministries.

Any understanding of the subject of faith has to start in the book of Hebrews, in particular chapter 11 which has been described as the "Hall of Fame of Faith".

"Without faith it is impossible to please Him, for he who comes to God must believe that He is, and that He is a rewarder of those who diligently seek Him" (Hebrews 11:6).

"Faith is the substance of things hoped for, the evidence of things not seen" (Hebrews 11:1).

"While we do not look at the things which are seen, but at the things which are not seen. For the things which are seen are temporary, but the things which are not seen are eternal" (2 Corinthians 4:18).

"For we walk by faith, not by sight" (2 Corinthians 5:7).

This is not about blind faith because it is predicated on the word of God and the witness of the Holy Spirit in those who are born again. It is only seeing through spiritual eyes that we can understand the working of faith, that is, revealing as a real fact what the natural man, being limited to his five senses, cannot always understand and accept.

If there is a scripture which challenges us to dig deep into the understanding of faith and its significance to our Christian walk it is, *"For whatever is born of God overcomes the world. And this is the victory that has overcome the world – our faith"* (1 John 5:4). This verse needs to be read in conjunction with John 16:33, *"These things I have spoken to you, that you may in Me have peace. In the world you will have tribulation, but be of good cheer, I have overcome the world."*

In this chapter I can do no more than alert seekers of the truth to the place of faith in our walk with Jesus and point them towards where they will receive teaching from those anointed by God to teach faith. (See the Acknowledgements for details of some of the ministries which move under such an anointing, and which I have found inspirational.)

CHAPTER 7

Exceedingly Great and Precious Promises

It was in Peter's second letter that I made another amazing discovery that had been hidden from me, which showed me the purpose of my life and my destination.

"Grace and peace be multiplied to you in the knowledge of God and of Jesus our Lord, as His divine power has given to us all things that pertain to life and godliness, through the knowledge of Him who called us by glory and virtue, by which have been given to us exceedingly great and precious promises, that through these you may be partakers of the divine nature, having escaped the corruption that is in the world through lust" (2 Peter 1:2-4).

There is so much of significance in these verses but overriding it all is the declaration of what "church" is all about, what is God's ultimate purpose in His plan for our salvation. There it is, *"that we might be partakers of the divine nature"*. That is what every Christian needs to understand and seek because it is his calling. It is attained through the *"exceedingly great and precious promises"*. In fact, it is more than a calling, it is the born-again believers right through the blood covenant.

This scripture tells me, in plain terms, that God has made a way for me to share in His divine nature; in other words, to become like Jesus. This is not some outrageous claim that I am making up; there is ample scriptural authority for making it.

Many Christians, if not most, are trying by their best efforts to be like Jesus. Who wouldn't? But I wonder how many know that God, through the blood covenant, has opened the way for them to achieve that sublime state without any effort on their part to earn it, because He has done it for them. Our only part is to understand and believe it and, by faith, receive it and act upon it.

Thus, as we gain an understanding of the promises, we will find ourselves potentially enjoying the same relationship with God as Adam, who, before his betrayal, was in a perfect spiritual relationship with the Father. I have heard it put another way, that God is restoring to us the blessing by God of His creation (Genesis 1:28) which was lost by Adam's fall. The world we are in remains fallen but we, His church, are commissioned (Mathew 28:18-20) to reclaim it.

The fundament truth of the blood covenant, which every believer must understand, is that by virtue of it God has made provision for him or her to be recreated to be like Jesus. In the following chapter I have set out what that provision is, if only we learn through teaching or study of the scriptures, to appropriate it to ourselves by faith. Three relevant scriptures are:

"For He made Him who knew no sin to be sin for us, that we might become the righteousness of God" (2 Corinthians 5:21).

"Love has been perfected among us in this: that we may have boldness in the day of judgment; because as He is, so are we in this world" (1 John 4:17).

"For in Him dwells all the fullness of the Godhead bodily; and you are complete in Him, who is the head of all principality and power" (Colossians 2:9-10).

All this I have had to find out for myself because in my seventy years in the church I cannot recall any teaching on this foundational truth, which answers the question of who I am, (who every born-again believer is), in Christ. "Daylight robbery" again springs to mind!

I have come to understand that the *"exceedingly great and precious promises"* work together to enable whoever seeks the truth, with all his heart, to find the way which Jesus has already opened to him, to bring him to the finishing line described by Paul.

"Not that I have already attained, or am already perfected; but I press on, that I may lay hold of that for which Christ Jesus has also laid hold of me" (Philippians 3:12).

CHAPTER 8

The Promises – Believing and Receiving

It is hard to know where to start with the exceedingly great and precious promises, which are backed by the blood covenant, because each one is both great and precious, and, working together, deliver a divine gift which challenges my comprehension of the length, breadth, height and depth of God's selfless love, which has made this provision for me at such great cost to Himself.

Eternal life is God's gift for His family members, to be enjoyed with the Father and Jesus in the kingdom of heaven. The promises are working together to accomplish that end for those who God calls to Himself, by preparing each of us for that privilege here and now, because we born-again believers are already in the kingdom of heaven.

"If you were of the world, the world would love its own. Yet because you are not of the world, but I chose you out of the world, therefore the world hates you," (John 15: 19).

By virtue of the blood covenant the process begins with our new birth. Scripture tells us, *"Now this I say, brethren, that flesh and blood cannot inherit the kingdom of God; nor does corruption inherit incorruption"* (1 Corinthians 15:50).

But *"giving thanks to the Father who has qualified us to be partakers of the inheritance of the saints in the light. He has delivered us from the power of darkness and conveyed us into the kingdom of the Son of His love, in whom we have redemption through His blood, the forgiveness of sins"* (Colossians 1:12-14).

Having been rescued from the power of the devil, that is the power of darkness, we see how through the promises, we have *"escaped the corruption that is in the world through lust"* (2 Peter 1:4). This is the result of the power of sin over us having been broken through Jesus' sacrifice in our place.

The flesh and blood problem obviously was, and always will be, a barrier to man's entry into the kingdom of heaven if he tries to qualify on his own merits and by his good works.

But the promise is that on our new birth we instantly become a new creation with the past wiped out, at the same time we are made the righteousness of God in Christ and Jesus enters our hearts by the Holy Spirit, so giving our inner reborn man a spiritual life and opening the door to our becoming partakers of the divine nature.

We become unrecognisable from the outward person we were before this, and inwardly we are brand-new creations reflecting the life of Jesus in us.

So, that is what happened to me in the spiritual realm when on that evening in 1984 I knelt on our sitting-room floor, repented of, and asked for forgiveness from Jesus for my many sins, acknowledged Him as my Lord and Saviour, and I invited Him into my heart.

That is when and how I was saved, and that is the exact moment when my life was transformed by what is called the divine exchange – His life for mine. I was rescued from the power of darkness; I became a new creation when my past was wiped out, and so much more, which I explore in the next chapter.

As with any new birth I had to grow up and learn to walk, which I have been doing over thirty-nine years. I am still grow-

The Promises – Believing and Receiving

ing into the understanding of what happened that night. This book seeks to share what scripture teaches of the new birth and how being born again transformed me and in many ways was experienced by me. Whilst my story, it seeks to share what is the inheritance of every "whoever" who is born again, because:

"... *as His divine power has given to us all things that pertain to life and godliness, through the knowledge of Him who called us by glory and virtue*" (2 Peter 1:3).

An early lesson for me was to understand that the verb "to believe" can mean different things to different people, who may each interpret it by their own lights.

I found one good but challenging definition: "A constant outlook of trust towards God whereby human beings abandon all reliance on their own efforts and put their full confidence in Him, His word and His promises." I can't remember where I sourced it, but I wrote it in the front of the Bible I was given on my licensing as a lay reader. That definition must raise the bar for many believers.

Equally important, I have learned, is what is the seeker's understanding of the full meaning and significance of what confessing the lordship of Jesus is going to involve. It is significant because unless the confession is backed up by a genuine, from the heart, intention to submit one's life to the lordship of Jesus, the words will be no more than that – empty. One, again challenging, definition of what the lordship of Jesus involves is: "For Jesus to be Lord of your life means that He is the ruler, the boss, the master of your whole life, not just a part.

He must be given control of the entire life." In short, summed up in the few words, "If Jesus is not Lord of all, He is not Lord at all," which is effectively shorthand for the fuller definition. In reality this definition must be for the more mature believer; it will be a process for the new believer to grow into.

As explained above, what happened instantly as I made my confession has been called "the divine exchange" where I gave Jesus my life and He gave me His as He entered my heart. Thus, I experienced, *"The mystery which has been hidden from ages and generations, but now has been revealed to His saints . . . which is Christ in you, the hope of glory"* (Colossians 1:26-27).

CHAPTER 9

What We Receive on Our New Birth

"Therefore, if anyone is in Christ, he is a new creation"
(2 Corinthians 5:17).

On my new birth I, as does every new-born believer, became *"a new creation"* (2 Corinthians 5:17) and became *"the righteousness of God in Him"* (2 Corinthians 5:21). Yes, I, Peter Spreckley, who had once been guilty of such sin, was now declared righteous in God's eyes, *"For He made Him who knew no sin to be sin for us, that we might become the righteousness of God in Him"* (2 Corinthians 5:21). I was made what I could not make myself. That's grace!

"Righteousness" is not the same as "holiness". Righteousness speaks of our right-standing with God from the moment we are born again. Holiness is manifested in our walk with Him by word, thought or deed, and is a life journey during which we are sanctified by Jesus (Hebrews 2:11), the Holy Spirit (1 Cor 6:11) and His word (John 17:17), as we move closer to God. I have never forgotten what a friend alerted me to, "The closer you get to the light the more blemishes you will see!" He was right!

Until 1984 I understood in theory, at least, that Jesus had taken my sin on the cross, so I did not have to pay the price for it, but the sad thing was that I had not received even the basic foundational teaching that I had to be born again of the Holy Spirit to become a Christian. It is not surprising that any promises however great and precious were unknown to me.

It followed that I, and indeed any seeker who is not taught the fundamental truths around being born again of the Holy Spirit, however sincere we might be, will not inherit all that is promised to us under the blood covenant.

This is because we would not be Christians, as was my case in 1984, despite all my years of going to church, my christening as an infant and confirmation at school when I was 15. While I had taken those steps which would seem to tick all the right boxes, I had not made a personal and informed decision of commitment of my life to Jesus as my Lord and Saviour, informed, that is, to the point of understanding and wanting above all else the implications of what I was doing.

But in 1984 I made that informed decision, and I was born again of the Holy Spirit as I made my confession of my many sins and surrendered my life to Jesus on our sitting-room floor. That released and made available to me all the promises of God, if I only received them by faith and, where appropriate, acted on them. The process of coming into an understanding of the promises was a process over the years as I spent time in the scriptures. This is what I now know;

I was instantly **"*rescued . . . from the kingdom of darkness and transferred . . . into the Kingdom of his dear Son*"** (Colossians 1:13 NLT). It was, I admit, a huge shock to me that all the time up to then (that is before my new birth), I had been under the control of the devil, because the scripture "*We know that we are of God, and the whole world lies under the sway of the wicked one*" (1 John 5:19) was unknown to me.

Indeed, there seems to be in the church, and outside, a belief of many that it is God who is in control of events occurring on the earth and therefore responsible for allowing, or indeed causing, all the terrible events we witness in the world.

God is indeed in ultimate control, but he delegated to Adam His authority to be exercised over the earth (Genesis 1:28), which Adam surrendered to the devil when he preferred the devil's word over God's word. Reclaiming the kingdom for Jesus is as already stated the commission of the church through its members.

My Spiritual eyes were opened. "Most assuredly, I say to you, unless one is born again, he cannot see the kingdom of heaven."

I am now in a relationship with God. He knows me and I know Him, no longer just about Him. God is Spirit and I needed a spiritual rebirth to have an intimate spiritual relationship with Him (see chapter 12).

I became a child of God, God now being my Father. How this happens is described in John's gospel where in the first chapter John writes of the response of the Jews to Jesus.

"The true Light which gives light to every man coming into the world . . . He came to His own, and His own did not receive Him. But as many as received Him, to them He gave the right to become children of God, to those who believe in His name: who were born, not of blood, nor of the will of the flesh, nor of the will of man, but of God" (John 1:9,11-13).

In other words, I was not a child of God until I was born again of the Holy Spirit.

I became a blood covenant brother of Jesus. Of the many surprises I have had on my spiritual journey, this must be one of the greatest. Me, a brother of Jesus? It can't be true, but it is! Think about it. He and the born-again me share the same Father through the Holy Spirit. So, looking at it through spiritual eyes, the answer is again, "Of course." How does Jesus see it?

"For both He who sanctifies and those who are being sanctified are all one, for which reason He is not ashamed to call them brethren" (Hebrews 2:11).

I am the temple of the Holy Spirit. *"Or do you not know that your body is the temple of the Holy Spirit who is in you, whom you have from God, and you are not your own?"* (1 Corinthians 6:19).

I am a citizen of heaven. *"For our citizenship is in heaven, from which we also eagerly wait for the Saviour, the Lord Jesus Christ"* (Philippians 3:20). Also, *"I do not pray that You should take them out of the world, but that You should keep them from the evil one. They are not of the world, just as I am not of the world"* (John 17:15-16).

I am no longer a sinner, and God no longer condemns me because as a new creation I am no longer infected by the sin nature which I, as we all do, inherited from our earthly father and which had separated me from God. Yes, of course I still sin and always will (which in Romans 3:23 is defined as *"falling short of the glory of God"* or "missing the mark"), even as a child of God, but my sin is covered and dealt with and forgotten because, *"There is therefore now no condemnation to those who are in Christ Jesus, who do not walk according to the flesh, but according to the Spirit"* (Romans 8:1) and, *"If we confess our sins, He is faithful and just to forgive us our sins and to cleanse us from all unrighteousness"* (1 John 1:9).

Our sin will not condemn us but, without repentance, will interrupt our relationship with the Father. Then, following our confession, He restores us to that right relationship.

This is because under the blood covenant, the blood of Jesus cleanses us from our sin instead of merely covering it, as was the case of the blood of sacrificed animals under the old covenant. If we are cleansed from all unrighteousness, then we are restored to the righteousness in Jesus we were given on our new birth.

I am a partaker of the divine nature (2 Peter 1:4).

I am being conformed to the image of Jesus. In other words, I am being changed to be like Jesus because *"For whom He foreknew, He also predestined to be conformed to the image of His Son, that He might be the firstborn among many brethren"* (Romans 8:29). And then I also know from Paul's letter to the Philippians that *"He who has begun a good work in you will complete it until the day of Jesus Christ"* (Philippians 1:6), that is, if I cooperate with Him. That is the trajectory for the rest of my life.

I have access to the throne room of heaven through prayer. Remembering that I am in a righteous relationship with the Lord, I can follow the admonition that we can *"come boldly to the throne of grace, that we may obtain mercy and find grace to help us in time of need"* (Hebrews 4:16).

I am filled with the fullness of God. *"For in Him dwells all the fullness of the Godhead bodily; and you are **complete in Him**, who is the head of all principality and power"* (Colossians 2:9-10).

I am filled with the power of God. *"For God has not given us a spirit of fear, but of **power** and of love and of a sound mind*" (2 Timothy 1:7). And *"He who is in you is greater than he who is in the world"* (1 John 4:4). (See chapter 19.), and *"Now to Him who is able to do exceedingly abundantly above all we ask or think, according to the power that works in us, to Him be glory in the church by Christ Jesus . . ."*

I am healed. "*Who Himself bore our sins in His own body on the tree, that we, having died to sins, might live for righteousness – by whose stripes you were **healed**"* (1 Peter 2:24). (See also chapter 22.)

I have the mind of Christ. (See chapter 5.)

I have not just abundant, but more abundant, life. "*The thief does not come except to steal, and to kill, and to destroy. I have come that they may have life, and that they may have it **more abundantly**"* (John 10:10).

The gifts of the Spirit as set out in 1 Corinthians 12 are available to us as we exercise whatever ministry God calls us to.

The fruit of the Spirit which is the divine nature: "*love, joy, peace, longsuffering, kindness, goodness, faithfulness, gentleness, self-control*" (Galatians 5:22-23) is imparted into our spirit on our new birth.

One thing we all must desire is peace. Jesus tells us, "***Peace I leave with you, My peace I give to you*** . . . *Let not your heart be troubled, neither let it be afraid*" (John 14:27).

Then in Philippians we are exhorted, "*Be anxious for nothing, but in everything by prayer and supplication, with thanksgiving, let your requests be known to God;* ***and the peace of God, which surpasses all understanding, will guard your hearts and minds through Christ Jesus***" (Philippians 4:6-7).

There is a neat shorthand for this: "*Therefore humble yourselves under the mighty hand of God, that He may exalt you in due time, casting all your cares upon Him, for He cares for you*" (1 Peter 5:6-7). The way up in the kingdom of heaven in down.

Faith. "*Looking unto Jesus, the author and finisher of our faith*" (Hebrews 12:2). Having received faith on my new birth

I do not need to ask for more, rather to exercise it by getting deeper into the word of God, because *"faith comes by hearing, and hearing by the word of God"* (Romans 10:17).

Paul writes, *"I have been crucified with Christ; it is no longer I who live, but Christ lives in me; and the life which I now live in the flesh I live by faith in the Son of God, who loved me and gave Himself for me"* (Galatians 2:20). Most versions of the Bible note that in this verse *"the faith **of** God"* is an alternative translation.

The above is a sample of the spiritual and life-changing provisions for us through the blood covenant which, as already shared above, made the resources of heaven available to those who have entered the kingdom of heaven through the new birth.

When I consider the extraordinary divine input into the spiritual life of the new-born Christian, which had such a profound impact on and in me by enabling me to serve God in a way which would have been unthinkable without that experience, I am astounded that the church seems so embarrassed by mention of the word "born-again", let alone understanding the foundational step it is in a believer's life to equip him or her for service of God.

One of the challenges arising from my understanding of the blood covenant and the promises was that my prayer life needed redirection. Often, what I had been asking God for I came to understand had already been given me. Jesus had said with His last breath on the cross, *"It is finished"*, which means that He has done all that is needed to be done for our complete salvation, not just saving us from the consequences of our sin. So, I was asking for what God had already provided for me.

God spoke to me about this when I was at an FGB meeting in Torquay some years ago. He spoke to me in the plainest terms and told me to share it with the men there. He has also told me to share it again at other meetings, "Stop asking me to do what I have already done and stop asking me to do what I have commanded you to do."

Sadly, I continue to hear prayers asking, for instance, for more faith, more power, healing and so forth. When we renew our minds as instructed to do in Romans 12:2 and read the scriptures through our spiritual eyes, we see that everything we need has been provided under the blood covenant, and resources which we are asking for are ours by virtue of the blood covenant to be received by faith.

This is why a full and accurate understanding the law of faith and how it works is so vital to our effectiveness as witnesses to an unbelieving world. (See chapter 6)

CHAPTER 10

The Word of God

> *"It is the Spirit who gives life; the flesh profits nothing. The words that I speak to you are spirit, and they are life"* (John 6:63).

Everyone who is searching for the truth about God must make a choice. The Bible contains the stories of two main covenants, both of which God has made, the first with Abraham (the old covenant) and then with Jesus, the new covenant for the eternal salvation of man, which the old covenant could not achieve. From the start I assumed that the Bible contained the inerrant word of God by which we are called to live.

Nevertheless, believing or not believing what is written in the Bible is a choice which anyone who opens it must make. What I can say is that as I have over the years been seeking God in the scriptures, I have found, to my legally trained mind at least, a compelling case for the Bible being the unchanging and infallible word of God. This is confirmed by the fact that faith in the written word of God has in so many ways led to my personal experience of the truth in that word.

It is faith in the word of God which leads to experience rather than the other way around. The word of God is backed by the blood covenant, and, as every lawyer will know, covenants cannot be unilaterally broken. They are binding on both parties, and, in the case of blood covenants, with terrible consequences for either party if they break it.

The ability for a believer to experience the word of God is made possible because, as Jesus says in John 6:63, *"It is the Spirit who gives life; the flesh profits nothing. The words that I speak to you are spirit, and they are life."* If they are living words, then we can experience them, and if Jesus' words are spirit, then they contain the power of the Holy Spirit. Without having had real experiences I would not have a story to tell.

So, I let the Bible speak for itself, at the same time reminding the reader that it is his or her choice whether to believe that the scriptures which I share, or indeed any other scriptures, are God speaking. I dare to suggest that it might be wise to read on before making the choice. It doesn't have to be "your final answer"!

I have already in chapter 6 remarked that Jesus anticipated that some might find it hard to believe what He was saying about the kingdom of heaven, so He gave us the key to believing, when He said, *"Assuredly, I say to you, whoever does not receive the kingdom of God as a little child will by no means enter it"* (Mark 10:15). This can be problematic for the not yet seeker who must rely on reason, which will find much of the Bible unbelievable. Scripture itself warns us in 1 Corinthians 2:14, *"But the natural man does not receive the things of the Spirit of God, for they are foolishness to him, nor can he know them, because they are spiritually discerned."*

Call me naïve, if you will, but that verse in Mark 10 describes my attitude towards the whole Bible, which I now know is the only way to receive the word of God. That is, "If my daddy says it, I believe it."

That attitude I have learned is to be maintained throughout our walk with the Lord. We don't have to worry or be embarrassed about having a childlike approach because this is covered by Paul, who explains, *"For since, in the wisdom of God, the world through wisdom did not know God, it pleased God through the foolishness of the message preached to save those who believe"* (1 Corinthians 1:21).

The following are just a few scriptures which are a window into what the Bible says about the word of God.

"In the beginning was the Word, and the Word was with God, and the Word was God. He was in the beginning with God. All things were made through Him, and without Him nothing was made that was made" (John 1:1-3).

"From childhood you have known the Holy Scriptures, which are able to make you wise for salvation through faith which is in Christ Jesus. All Scripture is given by inspiration of God and is profitable for doctrine, for reproof, for correction, for instruction in righteousness, that the man of God may be complete, thoroughly equipped for every good work" (2 Timothy 3:15-17).

As I read that scripture, I have to acknowledge that it is through faith in the word of God, and not my own efforts, which renders me *"complete"* and *"thoroughly equipped for every good work,"* and that *"every good work"* is that *"which God prepared beforehand that we should walk in them"* (Ephesians 2:10) and not my own ideas for helping God, however worthy they may seem.

"For the word of God is living and powerful, sharper than any two-edged sword, piercing even to the division of soul and spirit, and of joints and marrow, and is a discerner of the thoughts and intents of the heart" (Hebrews 4:12).

"My son, give attention to my words; incline your ear to my sayings. Do not let them depart from your eyes; keep them in the midst of your heart; for they are life to those who find them, and health to all their flesh" (Proverbs 4:20-22).

Believing the word of God is not without its challenges. (See chapter 27 to see what happened when I faced the ultimate challenge.)

"Man shall not live by bread alone; but man lives by every word that proceeds from the mouth of the Lord" (Deuteronomy 8:3). This scripture was confirmed by Jesus in His confrontation with the devil (Luke 4:4). For me it is the "Gold Standard" for the believer.

I accepted that Deuteronomy scripture to be how I must proceed, and, as best I can, I have sought to be obedient to that instruction. It was not like switching on a light, rather it is something I grew into as I progressed on my journey and spent more time in the word, with the result it has become a greater part of me.

The account of the encounter of Jesus with the devil in Luke 4 convinces me that the word of God is truly God speaking and, therefore, unchallengeable. In the account, the devil was facing his mortal enemy, and would have used any means to persuade Jesus to betray His Father. Yet Jesus, in answer, using *"the sword of the Spirit, which is the word of God"* (Ephesians 6:17) only had to say in response to the devil, *"It is written"*, and the devil was powerless to deny the truth of what was written, because he, the devil, was powerless against the word of God.

The devil's tactic with Eve had been to deceive her into disbelieving God's words to them. His tactic now is to deceive believers into doing the same thing. (See chapter 23 "The Narrow Gate and the Broad Gate")

One of the instant changes in my life after my rebirth was to develop a deep love of the word of God, leading to a great hunger to read it, which continues to this day. In short, I cannot get enough of it.

All those I know in the FGB and those in the church I attend who are reborn seem to have the same passion for the word of God. So, the disciplines of old, such as resolving to read so many chapters daily, are irrelevant. This is because if the words of the Bible are, in truth, God speaking through Jesus, whose words are *"spirit and life"*, they become, as it were, an essential part of our spiritual diet.

I end this chapter with God's instruction to Joshua in 1:8 when he was facing the challenge of leading the Israelites into the promised land, which is so relevant to those who *"seek first the kingdom of God and His righteousness"* (Mathew 6:33).

"This Book of Law shall not depart from your mouth, but you shall meditate on it day and night, that you may observe to do according to all that is written in it. For then you will make your way prosperous, and then you will have good success."

CHAPTER 11

Why Should I Believe Every Word that Proceeds from the Mouth of God?

"Let it be to me according to your word" (Luke 1:38).

In the previous chapter I have said that it is best to let the Bible speak for itself. There are so many scriptures revealing the characteristics of God's word but also how, in common parlance, the word and so the kingdom of heaven actually operate.

That is a bold claim, but in my thirty-nine years of searching the scriptures, I have found that as we mine for the riches in the word we find that God has revealed so much more about Himself and His "modus operandi", if you like, all of which emanates from His love for us and His desire that none should be lost but all come not only to a saving knowledge of Him, but to be like Jesus and come *"to the unity of faith and of the knowledge of the Son of God, to a perfect man, to the measure of the stature of the fullness of Christ; that we should no longer be children, tossed to and fro and carried about with every wind of doctrine . . . but, speaking the truth in love, may grow up in all things into Him who is the head – Christ* (Ephesians 4:13-15).

God Himself honours His word higher than His name, so how much more should we make His word our final authority?

"I will worship toward Your holy temple and praise Your name for Your loving kindness and Your truth; **for You have magnified Your word above all Your name**" (Psalm 138:2).

"Man shall not live by bread alone, but by every word that proceeds from the mouth of God" (Matthew 4:4).

The significance of the word and the need to believe it is highlighted in and by the parable of the sower. The parable speaks of sowing seeds, but Jesus in explaining the meaning of the parable calls the seed the "the word", *"The sower sows the word"* (Mark 4:14).

Jesus goes on to share that only the seed sown on good ground bears' fruit. *"The ones sown on good ground, those who hear the word, accept it, and bear fruit: some thirtyfold, some sixty, and some a hundred"* (Mark 4:20).

If we forget or ignore that we are called and appointed to bear "fruit that should remain" (John 15:16) we maybe find that our ministry is diminished with eternal consequences.

As I have committed myself to living by faith in the Mathew 4:4/Deuteronomy 8:3 command – yes, it is a command, it is a "shall" rather than a "should" – the authority for it must be in the word itself. This is what I find scripture tells me. This word is coming from God Himself through Jesus who tells us that He only speaks what He hears His Father saying.

"For I have not spoken on My own authority; but the Father who sent Me gave Me a command, what I should say and what I should speak. And I know that His command is everlasting life. Therefore, whatever I speak, just as the Father has told Me, so I speak" (John 12:49-50).

I read into those words that if God's words contain *"everlasting life"* there must be divine life which means divine power in the words.

This is confirmed by Jesus in John 6:63 when He says, *"The words that I speak to you are spirit, and they are life."* It is, after all, the power of the Holy Spirit that created light when Jesus spoke the word of God, *"Let there be light"* (Genesis 1:3), and it is the same *"exceeding greatness of His power toward us who believe, according to the working of His mighty power which He worked in Christ when He raised Him from the dead and seated Him at His right hand in the heavenly places"* (Ephesians 1:19-20).

So I believe, and I have witnessed, that the power of God is in His word because God Himself is watching over it to see that it achieves the purposes for which it is sent.

"You have seen well, for I am ready to perform My word" (Jeremiah 1:12).

"For as the rain comes down, and the snow from heaven, and do not return there, but water the earth, and make it bring forth and bud, that it may give seed to the sower and bread to the eater, so shall My word be that goes forth from My mouth; it shall not return to Me void, but it shall accomplish what I please, and it shall prosper in the thing for which I sent it" (Isaiah 55:10-11).

"God is not a man, that He should lie, nor a son of man, that He should repent. Has He said, and will He not do? Or has He spoken, and will He not make it good?" (Numbers 23:19).

I also love the verses in Proverbs 4:20-22 for further confirmation that God's word is living and powerful, and active in our health, when His word is alive in our heart and mind. *"My son, give attention to my words; incline your ear to my sayings. Do not let them depart from your eyes; keep them in the midst of your heart; for they are life to those who find them, and health to all their flesh."*

Finally, and perhaps conclusively, if God's plan for us under the blood covenant is that we become like Jesus (see chapter

12), then we will naturally want to do as Jesus did, which was to walk in absolute faith in every word which proceeded from the mouth of His Father. Can I achieve that? Certainly not, but I will seek to, so, "Yes, as best I can."

I cannot but think that the many problems which afflict the church are but a symptom of its failure to believe and act on *"every word that proceeds from the mouth of God"*. Nowhere in scripture are we given the licence to pick and choose which parts are to be believed. Indeed, if the church is truly the body of Christ on earth, then, again, are we not bound to speak, believe, and act on Jesus' words, as He did on His Father's words, and expect the same results, or even greater ones?

"Most assuredly, I say to you, he who believes in Me, the works I do he will do also; and greater works than these he will do, because I go to My Father" (John 14:12).

If anyone is in doubt about the need to obey the word of God, he needs to meditate on, *"He who has My commandments and keeps them, it is he who loves Me. And he who loves Me will be loved by My Father, and I will love him and manifest Myself to him"* (John 14:21).

A reminder of God's final word on this subject; *"Blessed are those who do His commandments, that they may have the right to the tree of life and may enter through the gates into the city"* (Revelation 22:14).

CHAPTER 12

Why I Must Be Born Again

"Do not marvel that I said to you, 'You must be born again'" (John 3:7).

I do not recall any teaching on this question. Indeed, as I have already mentioned, when I started my journey of discovery in the library in 1984, I had no understanding of what being born again meant, let alone its significance.

The obvious answer to the question "Why must I be born again?" is because Jesus tells me and every seeker why.

"This man came to Jesus by night and said to Him 'Rabbi, we know that You are a teacher come from God; for no one can do these signs that You do unless God is with him.' Jesus answered and said to him, 'Most assuredly, I say to you, unless one is born again, he cannot see the kingdom of God.' Nicodemus said to Him, 'How can a man be born when he is old? Can he enter a second time his mother's womb and be born?' Jesus answered, 'Most assuredly, I say to you, unless one is born of water and the Spirit, he cannot enter the kingdom of God. That which is born of the flesh is flesh, and that which is born of the Spirit is spirit. Do not marvel that I said to you, "You must be born again"'" (John 3:2-7).

Another compelling reason for being born again is that unless we experience a new birth we are not a Christian. It follows that none of the exceedingly great and precious promises is available. Our religious fervour simply does not count.

"Now if anyone does not have the Spirit of Christ, he is not His" (Romans 8:9).

The process of being born again is well illustrated in the first chapter of the same gospel when St John, in that well-known ninth lesson in the pre-Christmas carol service, writes:

"He was in the world, and the world was made through Him, and the world did not know Him. He came to His own, and His own did not receive Him. But as many as received Him, to them He gave the right to become children of God, to those who believe in His name: who were born, not of blood, nor of the will of the flesh, nor of the will of man, but of God" (John 1:10-13).

I found this description helpful in understanding what is happening in the rebirth by the Holy Spirit. Nicodemus was about as religious as a man could be, but he could not, in his human mind, understand the spiritual truth that Jesus was sharing.

There is one aspect to the need to be born again which I have never heard addressed in sermons and that is in Revelation chapter 20, which I discovered as I searched the scriptures.

"And I saw the dead, small and great, standing before God, and books were opened. And another book was opened, which is the Book of Life. And the dead were judged according to their works, by the things which were written in the books. The sea gave up the dead who were in it, and Death and Hades delivered up the dead who were in them. And they were judged, each one according to his works. Then Death and Hades were cast into the lake of fire. This is the second death. And anyone not found written in the Book of Life was cast into the lake of fire" (Revelation 20:12-15).

Why I Must Be Born Again

There seems to be no dispute that the Book of Life, which I had never even heard of, contains the names of those who have been redeemed by the blood of Jesus, those born again, who are family members. It's the family album. Jesus Himself tells the seventy disciples, when they return from their mission:

"Behold, I give you authority . . . over all the power of the enemy, and nothing shall by any means hurt you. Nevertheless do not rejoice in this, that the spirits are subject to you, but rather rejoice because your names are written in heaven" (Luke 10:19-20).

Who are those whose names are written in the Book of Life but those who have been born again into the family of God? No wonder the well-known American evangelist Charles Finney (1792–1875) when asked why he was always preaching the need to be born again replied, "Because you need to be born again."

It's surprising and even sad to me that over all the time, 1984 to date, I have had an interest in how the church is regarded by the world outside, there has been a perceived understanding of "born-again" Christians, that they are fanatics and do not represent the "orthodox" Christian faith.

Within the church as well, in my experience as a lay reader, the very term "born again" can be a non-subject or cause embarrassment. If only the church would be open about this pre-condition to becoming a Christian, and taught this truth to those in its care, because if we have not been born again Christ is not in us and so we are not Christians.

There is another reason why a believer must be born again. God is spirit (John 4:24) and He reveals Himself through His words which are spirit and are life (John 6:63). To receive

His words, we need to have a receiver capable of receiving spiritual truths.

On receipt of the Holy Spirit, which occurs on our new birth, He becomes our "spiritual receiver", and so our eyes of faith are opened.

Until then, however religious and sincere we have been, Jesus will not know us, that is spirit to spirit intimacy, and we will be no better off than the unfortunate bridesmaids or the wonderworkers referred to in chapter 16. Of course he knew them as humans created in His own image, as He knows every person who walks this earth, but the spirit in each had not been given new birth.

I am trusting that my story will be an example of how any "whoever" who seeks God wholeheartedly, believes God unconditionally, and obeys God faithfully by following His word in scripture, can be used by God to make a difference, because God already has plans for him or her to do so.

"For we are His workmanship, created in Christ Jesus for good works, which God prepared beforehand that we should walk in them" (Ephesians 2:10).

There is laid down in scripture the order in which we are brought by God to where we are equipped to carry out the "good works" which we are created for; first, repentance towards God, next, faith in Jesus (the new birth when we are recreated in Him), followed by baptism in water and baptism in the Holy Spirit (the power which was first given to the church at Pentecost).

That is how I was delivered from the power of darkness into the kingdom of heaven where I now have citizenship and have been equipped by God to do the works which I was created for, which I touch on in this book. It is what Jesus has chosen me for. Every believer has a calling, but no two are the same.

"You did not choose Me, but I chose and appointed you that you should go and bear fruit, and that your fruit should remain, that whatever you ask the Father in My name He may give you" (John 15:16).

CHAPTER 13

The Level Playing Field

"But God has chosen the foolish things of the world to put to shame the wise" (1 Corinthians 1:27).

I had until 1984 accepted that it is only ordained ministers in the church who have all the theology to stand at the front and teach, and that what they said must be "gospel truth". How wrong I was. I can say that because no one had taught me about the level playing field God has laid down, which ensures that no one starts with what we would naturally consider to be an advantage in our pursuit of Him.

In fact, I found that in God's economy some people do have such an advantage, but it is not those I would have expected to be advantaged. I found this in the first letter to the Corinthians where in the first chapter I read:

"Remember, dear brothers and sisters, that few of you were wise in the world's eyes or powerful or wealthy when God called you. Instead, God chose things the world considers foolish in order to shame those who think they are wise. And he chose things that are powerless to shame those who are powerful. God chose things despised by the world, things counted as nothing at all, and used them to bring to nothing what the world considers important. As a result, no one can ever boast in the presence of God" (1 Corinthians 1:26-29 NLT).

So, I had to learn that God is countercultural, and I found great comfort in the revelation that I could count myself among the foolish. This means that there is no barrier to our coming into as good an understanding, if not better, of the gospel and God's revelation of Himself compared with the wisest theologian, if the Holy Spirit is our teacher.

Nevertheless, God has ordained men and women with a special anointing to teach general or specific aspects of faith whose wisdom, experience, and teaching can take us from where we are to an even deeper understanding of and participation in our full redemption. An early lesson for me was that the way up in the kingdom of God is down.

"Therefore humble yourselves under the mighty hand of God, that He may exalt you in due time" (1 Peter 5:6).

I also learned that if I took my questions direct to God, He would always answer them, usually through scripture or perhaps a teaching video. There have been occasions when I have been wondering about some aspect of what I had been learning when, even before I had asked God about it, He answered or confirmed my thoughts.

One amazing example of this happened some years ago when I was wondering about the role of the Holy Spirit on earth today compared to when God spoke and the world was created, as recounted in Genesis. I went to a convention of FGB in Panama where one morning I was passing a table and was invited to sit down by a man who I had never met before. As we were introducing ourselves, he stopped and said, "Peter, God would say to you, 'God said, "Let there be light," and there was light.'" It was exactly what I had been wondering about back in England.

CHAPTER 14

Travellers' Joy

"For you see your calling, brethren, that not many wise according to the flesh . . . are called"
(1 Corinthians 1:26).

In this chapter I want to skip to the episode which occurred in a summer in about 1987. The exact date is not important. It underlines how God is countercultural.

At the relevant time there was a national media campaign against a group of people who were identified as "travellers". They were not gypsies but for the summer, at least, treated the countryside as open and available to them. They lived in vans of various types and moved in groups, occupying private land or public spaces at will, without respect for the place they were occupying, and often trashing those places before leaving. Not surprisingly, the public turned against them and the police were tasked to get rid of them, which they did, mainly by impounding their vehicles.

I was contacted by Vic Jacopson who ran and still runs a Christian ministry called Hope Now which was and still is involved in Ukraine. He was one of the few who were anxious to support the travellers. He contacted me to ask whether we would help some travellers who were at risk of losing their vehicles, by letting them park in our farmyard at our home in West Sussex. We agreed without any understanding of what it might involve. So started one of the strangest episodes in our life.

Dave was the first to arrive in an old van that turned out to have engine problems, meaning he was unable to leave us until it became road worthy – nearly two months later! He was followed by Looney (we never knew his proper name), Dave's girlfriend, Carol, who was pregnant but not by Dave, and Alistair. From time to time they were visited by friends.

On Dave's first day we invited him to eat with us. After he had had a bath, we fed him. Then I shared the gospel with him. He said he wanted to accept Jesus into his life, and when we prayed for him, the Holy Spirit fell on him for several minutes as he sat on our sofa. When he "came round" he told us that he had had a vision of Jesus.

Looney arrived the next day. The first words Dave greeted him with were, "I've been born again." We gave Looney the same welcome we had given Dave and his response to the gospel was the same as Dave's. Again, when we prayed the Holy Spirit fell, this time on both Looney and Dave, who were both sitting on our sofa. Again, it was many minutes later before they were able to speak.

I will pass over the many days when having the travellers in our yard was not easy or convenient, especially the day when Carol began to give birth. It shouldn't have been a problem except the locum GP, who was serving in the Navy, had less experience of dealing with a birth than Mary. When I asked him later what he had been doing in the Navy, he told me he had been mainly looking after constipated submariners! Mary got Carol to the nursing home in the nick of time.

Alistair was the third one to commit his life to Jesus. He is memorable because when he was with us, he had a dog which had been injured in a camp dog fight. Shortly after he left to return home, he telephoned me, which was a surprise. He wanted to tell me that on his way home, hitch-hiking, he was walking along the road, worrying about his dog. What he said next I have never forgotten, so I quote it verbatim. "I was worried about my dog, so I prayed to my heavenly Father [of 48 hours] and said, 'I need a vet,' and the first car that stopped was a vet and he has taken my dog to his surgery in Cambridge."

One day when I was in the garden, I was approached by Dave who told me that they had a problem. It was that they were trying to explain their encounter with Jesus to some friends who were visiting, but they were having difficulty in explaining things to them. I joined them in a granary room in the yard. There were at least six men crowded into the room. After my sharing the gospel and invitation to the visitors to turn to Christ, the Holy Spirit fell again and this time I was surrounded by the men under His power on the floor, again for several minutes.

It must have been quite a picture if anyone had looked in. Here I was, a respectable partner in a local solicitor's firm, surrounded by these men on the floor under the power of the Spirit. They were dressed in the travellers' dress code of denims, boots without laces, unwashed hair and mainly unshaven. "What on earth is going on?" I would have been asked. "It's heaven coming to earth," I would have replied.

Why do I tell you this story? Well, it seems to me to be a real-life parable. These young men were in many ways just like every other young man of their age, but when it came to a life-transforming decision to surrender their life to Jesus, they had a great advantage over many others of us when we are challenged to do the same.

They had no social standing where they needed to consider their position or reputation; they had no background of church and its traditions; and they had no worldly goods which they had to protect. They had little more with them than an old van, a saucepan and a camping stove. They relied on social welfare.

In other words, there were no reasons to think "What about . . .?" which can affect our response to the call of Jesus. They were effectively empty vessels open to the filling of the Holy Spirit. I believe that is what I witnessed. In other words, they were really like little children, fully accepting and without challenge, which is how we are all called to be.

They remained in touch with us for a short while when we heard that some of them had been baptised by Vic Jacopson in a cattle trough. Vic recently told me that he has remained in touch with them, and they have continued to follow Jesus, except Dave who has gone home to be with Him.

CHAPTER 15

The Will of God – Finding It

"May the God of peace . . . make you complete in every good work to do His will" (Hebrews 13:20-21).

This is another fundamental truth on which I received no teaching, yet ignorance of it could lead us into deep trouble. I say that because the gospels reveal several sayings of Jesus where He is stressing the importance of doing the will of His Father and at the same time issuing a warning of the consequences of not doing so.

"Not everyone who says to Me, 'Lord, Lord,' shall enter the kingdom of heaven, but he who does the will of My Father in heaven" (Matthew 7:21).

"My mother and My brothers are those who hear the word of God and do it" (Luke 8:21).

We need to know what the word of God says about doing His will. This is how we find His will:

"And do not be conformed to this world, but be transformed by the renewing of your mind, that you may prove what is that good and acceptable and perfect will of God" (Romans 12:2).

Renewing our mind is a choice, even though we may be born again. But if, after our new birth, we stay faithful to scripture, we will start to see through eyes of faith (see chapter 5) and the scriptures relevant to God's will start to speak to us. His will for us already exists; we just need to discover it. Jesus also speaks of the need to remain faithful to scripture in John 8:31 how *"abiding in My word"* leads to true discipleship – *"My disciples indeed"* – and thereby *"knowing the truth"* which *"makes you free."*

"Then Jesus said to those Jews who believed Him, "If you abide in my word, you are my disciples indeed. And you shall know the truth, and the truth shall make you free.""

That is God's will for each of us.

"For we are His workmanship, created in Christ Jesus for good works, which God prepared beforehand that we should walk in them" (Ephesians 2:10).

God has an individual plan for every believer, and it is up to each of us to seek God for it. If we fail to do that then we can be working ourselves into the ground believing we are serving Him, yet we could be outside His will; our best efforts fall into the category of "wood, hay, straw" and burn up when tested by fire (1 Corinthians 3:12-13).

Some time ago I listened to the testimony of an Indian pastor, Pastor Dhinakaran. His story contains an episode which is enlightening about how we can deceive ourselves into thinking we are doing God's will when we are not doing so. His story starts with him, a young man, heading for the nearest railway line with the intention of committing suicide. On the way he encountered a Christian lady who persuaded him to turn around and she led him to the Lord. He had at the time, it would seem according to his testimony, an encounter with Jesus and thereafter, over the years, he had further such meetings when the two of them would just talk. The pastor at the time worked in a bank whilst at the same time ministering the gospel.

One day in a meeting with Jesus, Jesus asked him whether he would give up his day job and work for Him full time. The pastor said, "No." Jesus asked him why, and the pastor said that it was because he had noticed that those who were working full time for Jesus were always poor.

The response to that (which I have never forgotten and why I am telling this story) was, "I didn't ask them to." That brings to mind those who said to Jesus, "*Lord, Lord, have we not prophesied in Your name, cast out demons in Your name, and done many wonders in Your name?*" who were told to depart and called "*you who practise lawlessness*" (Matthew 7:22-23).

The pastor did go full time and went on to build a huge ministry in India and further afield, and he also founded a university. He went to be with his Lord in 2008, but the ministry continues.[4]

We must beware of having our own agenda and sharing the fate of the wonderworkers in Matthew 7. We do this by seeking God's will, and exclusively moving in it.

"*See then that you walk circumspectly, not as fools but as wise, redeeming the time, because the days are evil. Therefore do not be unwise, but understand what the will of the Lord is*" (Ephesians 5:15-17).

As I have already mentioned, in my BC life, helping was my sole motivation. I believe that I thought that going to church was my way of pleasing God, and helping in church in the way

---

[4] www.jesuscallsministries.org

I did was doing likewise. How ignorant I was, but there was no teaching on that fundamental truth. Surely here and elsewhere, as I have since discovered, it was a case of the blind leading the blind, which Jesus said in Luke 6:39 had unfortunate consequences for both.

CHAPTER 16
Knowing God

And this is eternal life, that they may know You, the only true God, and Jesus Christ whom You have sent" (John 17:3).

One of the exceedingly great and precious promises flowing from the blood covenant is, as I have mentioned in chapters 8 and 12, that through our new birth we have an intimate relationship with the Father because our reborn spirit can communicate intimately with God who is spirit. In this chapter I explore how our knowing God, not just knowing about God, is so fundamental to our salvation.

Our intimate relationship with the Lord is defined by Paul in 1 Corinthians 6:17. It was written in the context of sexual relations between a man and a harlot, but the truth of what he is saying defines our relationship with Him after our new birth.

"But he who is joined to the Lord is one spirit with Him."

Going back to the evening when, during the time I was a churchwarden, I was driving to a meeting with our then vicar, I told him that I was worried about the passage in Matthew 7:21-23:

"Not everyone that says to Me, 'Lord, Lord,' shall enter the kingdom of heaven, but he who does the will of My Father in heaven. Many will say to Me on that day, 'Lord, Lord, have we not prophesied in Your name, cast out demons in Your name,

and done many wonders in Your name?' And then I will declare to them, 'I never knew you; depart from Me you who practise lawlessness!"

The vicar responded, "Don't worry about that. Concentrate on being a churchwarden." Well, I did worry about that, and in due course I found the answer in the Bible, of course! At the time I was seriously worried about the answer of Jesus, *"I never knew you; depart from Me you who practise lawlessness!"* to those who seemed to be doing what He would have wanted them to do. I also became concerned about the similar answer of Jesus recorded in Matthew chapter 25 in the story of the wise and unwise bridesmaids expanded below.

The starting point for discovering the meaning and significance of "knowing God" is in John 17:1-3, which form part of what is called Jesus' High Priestly Prayer. Jesus again speaking:

"Father, the hour has come. Glorify Your Son, that Your Son also may glorify You, as You have given Him authority over all flesh, that He should give eternal life to as many as You have given Him. And this is eternal life, that they may know You, the only true God, and Jesus Christ whom You have sent."

So, it is made clear that the definition of eternal life is "knowing God". That is the intimate relationship between God the Father and Jesus, His Son. The man or woman who has not been born again has not received the gift of eternal life, and so, as happened to the unprepared bridesmaids as described below, remains on the outside, only knowing about God.

I was amazed when I discovered that the Greek word for "know" in John 17:3 has the same meaning as in Genesis 4:1, *"And Adam knew Eve his wife, and she conceived."* That is the degree of intimacy open to us with our heavenly Father, and which we enjoy as soon as we have been born again of the Holy Spirit, because God is a Spirit (John 4:24). It is the same relationship Adam had with God before the fall.

Understanding this relationship, which is another foundational teaching I had not received, makes sense of what seems such a harsh response of the bridegroom in the parable of the ten bridesmaids in Mathew 25, as well as the workers of wonders in Matthew 7. When the unwise bridesmaids turned up late, having had to buy oil for their lamps, and were knocking at the locked door calling, *"'Lord, Lord, open to us!' But he answered and said, 'Assuredly, I say to you, I do not know you.'"*

There is really nothing difficult to understand here when one reads in Colossians where Paul is talking about *"the mystery which has been hidden from ages and from generations, but now has been revealed to His saints. To them God willed to make known what are the riches of the glory of this mystery among the Gentiles: which is Christ in you, the hope of glory"* (Colossians 1:26-27).

In Romans 8 Paul confirms this: *"So then, those who are in the flesh cannot please God. But you are not in the flesh but in the Spirit, if indeed the Spirit of God dwells in you. Now if anyone does not have the Spirit of Christ, he is not His"* (Romans 8:8-9).

Christ in you, and you know God and He knows you. Christ not in you, however sincere you are, the best you can do is know about God, and here lies the difference between religion and faith. In the simplest and, perhaps, crudest terms, this can be defined by religion being man's best efforts, by whichever way he chooses, to please and satisfy God, and so earn his salvation.

Faith is when man understands that he can never satisfy God by his own efforts to meet God's standards to achieve his salvation, but believes in and accepts God's free gift revealed through Jesus Christ.

As the definition by Paul in Romans 8:9 above defines a Christian as someone in whom Christ is living through the Holy Spirit, so on our rebirth instantly we are in a relationship with God because, again, " *For he who is joined to the Lord is one spirit with Him*" (1 Corinthians 6:16).

So, Christianity becomes a relationship with Jesus living in us, which distinguishes us from every other religion.

CHAPTER 17

The Kingdom of Heaven

> *"But seek first the kingdom of God and His righteousness, and all these things shall be added to you"* (Matthew 6:33).

I have never received teaching on the kingdom of heaven. Its existence seems to be taken for granted. The first surprise I had when I started searching was that there is another kingdom apart from the kingdom of heaven.

"We know that we are of God, and the whole world lies under the sway of the wicked one" (1 John 5:19).

How did that come about? As already explained in chapter 9 it is the result of God having given Adam *"dominion over the fish of the sea, over the birds of the air, and over every living thing that moves on the earth"* (Genesis 1:28).

God had thereby surrendered His own authority over the earth to Adam. When Adam fell for the serpent's – the devil's – deception and doubted God's word that he would surely die if he ate the fruit of the tree of the knowledge of good and evil, but instead believed the devil, then Adam forfeited his authority to the devil. The earth then became the devil's kingdom until the Son of Man – Jesus – came to rescue us by destroying the devil's authority and "opening the kingdom of heaven to all believers" (the *Te Deum*).

"The time is fulfilled, and the kingdom of God is at hand. Repent, and believe in the gospel" (Mark 1:15).

"Giving thanks to the Father who has qualified us to be partakers of the inheritance of the saints in the light. He has delivered us from the power of darkness and conveyed us into the kingdom of the Son of His love, in whom we have redemption through His blood, the forgiveness of sins" (Colossians 1:12-14).

I had to learn that there are indeed two kingdoms: the kingdom of heaven and the kingdom of Satan. We absolutely must understand this fact to make sense of what we see going on around us, both within and outside the church and worldwide.

Where are these two kingdoms? In the spirit world where we cannot see them through our physical eyes, but where we can through spiritual eyes.

The kingdom of Satan is where he rules. The kingdom of heaven is where Jesus, not the devil, is Lord, and that is in the hearts and lives of those in whom He is living, corporately, the church. That is why Jesus becoming our Lord is a fundamental condition of our salvation when, as described in chapter 9, we have the presence of the Holy Spirit in us, we have the fullness of God in us, the power of God in us, and we have authority over all the works of the devil. He who is in us is greater than he who is in the world.

"You are of God, little children, and have overcome them, because He who is in you is greater than he who is in the world" (1 John 4:4).

No wonder the devil hates Christians! No wonder Jesus encourages us in Matthew 6:32-33, *"For all these things the Gentiles seek. For your heavenly Father knows that you need all these things. But seek first the kingdom of God and His righteousness, and all these things shall be added to you."*

This was necessary because it was and is only when we receive the new birth, and are born again into the kingdom of heaven, that we inherit the promises of the blood covenant (see chapter 4), where all the resources of heaven become available to us in Jesus. Also, there is a spiritual reason why we need a spiritual birth. *"Now this I say, brethren, that flesh and blood cannot inherit the kingdom of God; nor does corruption inherit incorruption"* (1 Corinthians 15:50).

That is why our new birth becomes a condition precedent to our entry to God's kingdom. He has provided under the blood covenant that we become new creations, the righteousness of God in Christ, and so welcomed into the kingdom of heaven, which can only occur when we are born again. Our knowing God in a personal way through Jesus is a foundational step.

"Grace and peace be multiplied to you in the knowledge of God and of Jesus our Lord, as His divine power has given to us all things that pertain to life and godliness, through the knowledge of Him who called us by glory and virtue, by which have been given to us exceedingly great and precious promises, that through these you may be partakers of the divine nature" (2 Peter 1:2-4).

Paul tells us that *"the kingdom of God is not eating and drinking, but righteousness and peace and joy in the Holy Spirit"* (Romans 14:17). That is something to look forward to, and the kingdom is open to all who choose life rather than death.

I was never taught that on my new birth I become a citizen of heaven (see chapter 9). *"For our citizenship is in heaven, from which we also eagerly wait for the Saviour, the Lord Jesus Christ"* (Philippians 3:20).

Many people I have come across seem to be under the impression that it is only when we get to heaven that we will enjoy the benefits of healing. That will be true for those believers who have not understood that the benefits (see chapter 4) won for us by Jesus under the blood covenant are for us who have been born again. Those benefits are the "lifeblood" of the Christian now.

When Jesus does come for us, Paul goes on to explain, then we will be given new bodies which will be conformed to Jesus' "glorious body", but He has not come yet, and He has not left us to suffer in the meanwhile. To believe he has done so is to ignore, or simply not to believe, Jesus' wonderful promise that he has come *"that they may have life, and that they may have it more abundantly"* (John 10:10) by Himself bearing our sicknesses and diseases in the same way that He has borne our sin (see chapter 22).

CHAPTER 18

The Full Gospel Business Men's Fellowship International (FGB)

> *"Go into all the world and preach the gospel to every creature"* (Mark 16:15).

As I have already mentioned, after the meeting in Portsmouth Guildhall in 1984 I felt compelled to join that Fellowship. I rang their secretary the next day and drove twenty miles or more to join, there and then. God must have really wanted me to join them!

Shortly afterwards I went to one of their dinner meetings in Portsmouth. The speaker was Professor Roy Peacock who had been a professor of aeronautical science at Cambridge. His story was recorded in his book *Foolish To Be Wise*.

Yet again I fell to my knees and gave my life to Jesus and then went up for prayer. To my amazement he started to tell me that he had a picture of me walking across a plain saying, "Thus says the Lord." This was my first experience of anyone giving a prophetic word, and what he was saying was so far from how I was at that time – no more than a baby in the Lord – it meant absolutely nothing to me. But God . . .!

Soon afterwards I went to a prayer meeting of the Portsmouth chapter. I found myself in a room full of men from various walks of life praising God with a passion which I found embarrassing as I sat silently in the corner wondering what on earth I had got myself into. Then it got worse. They started praying to God and then for each other openly, loudly and enthusiastically, at times in a language that seemed meaningless, as if they knew who they were speaking to. And they were so happy!

I was so glad to go home but, nevertheless, I went back the next week and, again, I sat in the corner, dumbstruck by seeing the love for God and for each other expressed in this way. I had never experienced anything like it, and indeed I did not know, after my nearly forty years of church going, that it was possible. It certainly was not yet for me. At that stage I had not comprehended what had happened to these on-fire men. It was that their lives had been transformed by being born again and baptised in the Holy Spirit (see chapter 20).

Over the coming months I became accustomed to what was happening in the prayer meetings and gradually found it easier to praise God and pray with them, but the Anglican reserve in me continued to hold me back. I was, of course, still a baby Christian but at least I was receiving good spiritual food and was, over time, moving from the milk to more solid spiritual food.

At the same time, I did learn as I "grew up" in the Fellowship and received good teaching from men who truly knew the word of God and spoke out of experience, that the life of a Christian can be, even ought to be, much more exciting than anything I had experienced or witnessed. I learned that lives can only be transformed by the new birth and baptism in the Holy Spirit. Here was living proof.

These men, and almost all the other men I met over the years in the Fellowship, were ordinary people with no theological training and with ordinary jobs, yet they knew God in a very personal way. He talked to them, and they talked to Him.

The Full Gospel Business Men's Fellowship International (FGB)

When they prayed, things often happened. Expectations were high. If it was in the Bible, they believed it and expected it to happen.

They exercised the gifts of the Spirit as listed in chapter 12 of the first letter to the Corinthians. Later I came to exercise, and still do, some of those gifts as I grew in my spiritual knowledge and gained the confidence to step out of my comfort zone to seek to exercise them, when in the circumstances it was/is appropriate.

The vision for the Fellowship was very simple. The founder Demos Shakarian, having cried out to God, "Where are all the men in church?" was given a vision whereby the gospel would be shared by laymen telling their stories outside a church setting, often at lunches or dinners hosted by a chapter (the local group), but also to friends and families and to others they might meet.

They shared how they were before coming to faith, how they had come to faith and how their lives had changed as a result. Demos Shakarian's story and the story of the birth of the Fellowship, which would soon be established in over 100 nations, is recounted in the book *The Happiest People on the Earth*.[5]

It became a most effective and simple way of witnessing, and we had, and still have, *Voice Magazine*, which contains short testimonies from members, to give to anyone we meet. This was a calling outside our church life, but we were encouraged, as I did, to stay in our church and to give priority to supporting the church financially.

---

[5] Demos Shakarian with Elizabeth and John Sherrill, *The Happiest People on Earth: The Story of Demos Shakarian* (Hodder & Stoughton, 1996).

The "Full Gospel" part of the Fellowship's name is to signify that if it is in the Bible, we believe it. "Business Men" indicated that members would be working men in the widest sense. In 1952 women were not, in America at least, a major part of the workforce. "International" covered the world for our harvest field.

What was special, but in no way exclusive to the Fellowship, was the belief in and the reliance on the baptism of the Holy Spirit to equip members for the exercise of the ministry in the power of the Holy Spirit. I cover this in chapter 19.

The actual Statement of Faith of the Fellowship contains the following:

"We believe in the Baptism of the Holy Spirit accompanied by the initial sign of speaking in other tongues as the Spirit of God gives utterance (Acts 2:4), as distinct from the new birth, and in the nine gifts of the Holy Spirit listed in 1 Corinthians 12 as now available to believers."

The exemplar of "Full Gospel" ministry is Paul who wrote:

"For I will not dare to speak of any of those things which Christ has not accomplished through me, in word and deed, to make the Gentiles obedient – in mighty signs and wonders, by the power of the Spirit of God, so that from Jerusalem and round about to Illyricum I have fully preached the gospel of Christ" (Romans 15:18-19).

The doctrine of Baptism in the Holy Spirit is controversial, especially the concept of speaking in other tongues. I have read or listened to senior clergy in the church and pastors of other churches arguing why the Baptism of the Holy Spirit does not exist.

The Full Gospel Business Men's Fellowship International (FGB)

What is a significant part of my story is that, without question, I was baptised in the Holy Spirit (the proper translation is "baptised in spirit") when the power of God fell on me as I listened at home to the recording of the Guildhall meeting, after which I stood up transformed in so many ways, some very personal but particularly in my approach to my new-found faith.

From that moment on I became very bold in sharing the good news of Jesus Christ, becoming an embarrassment to some at home and in the local church! My confidence led me to start to pray for other people with needs.

I remember praying for a client of mine, David, who had broken his arm and was clutching it to his body on account of the pain. We were on our way to a conference with a barrister in London. I stopped the car and prayed for the healing of the broken arm, and then drove on. During the conference I was amazed to see David lean across the desk and pick up a pile of papers with the broken and painful arm! He told me on the way home that the arm was working normally and was pain free.

During my time in the Fellowship, I have travelled to many parts of the UK, sharing my testimony and ministering to those attending who asked for prayer. Further afield I have travelled in Europe and to countries in Africa, where I have shared my testimony at functions, taught in local churches, prayed for the sick and have seen many who said that they were healed.

This was in Egypt, where my colleague Paul and I were hustled out of a church before the police arrived as we should not have been there. In Kenya, where I ministered in the slums of Nairobi as well as remote villages. I have never forgotten arriving at a church and seeing the women brewing tea for the congregation in an old wheelbarrow

On one occasion I was ministering at a pastors' conference when there was a powerful move of the Holy Spirit, and many were touched to the point of weeping and crying out to God. In Tanzania, where my colleague Kevin and I found ourselves illegal immigrants in Zanzibar, which happily was resolved without any consequences.

In South Africa, I ministered in Johannesburg, Port Elizabeth, and Cape Town. What touched me most in the African visits was the openness of the people to the gospel and their passionate praying as they assailed heaven. Many churches there have dedicated Friday nights to all-night prayer meetings.

I record these experiences to show how a "whoever" who comes to God unconditionally, believes the whole word of God, and makes himself or herself available to Him, can be used by Him, because God already has a plan for that person's life.

My story is partly about how God was able to use me once I sought Him with all my heart, but more particularly about how believing and acting on the word of God transformed my life as I experienced the living word which is *"life and spirit"* being manifested in my life.

"For we are His workmanship, created in Jesus for good works, which God prepared beforehand that we should walk in them" (Ephesians 2:10).

So it was that I found myself in a world that, not so long before, I did not know existed.

My spiritual journey continued in FGB while I continued to attend our local church, which was next door to our home in West Sussex. One thing I had to learn was that the congregation were not enthusiastic about someone having an experience of

The Full Gospel Business Men's Fellowship International (FGB)

God, such as I had been privileged to have and tried to share. The same vicar who didn't want to explore the Matthew 7 warnings mentioned earlier, told me it could be "very dangerous".

However, in my enthusiasm and excitement and new boldness I started arranging a series of meetings in the parish to share what had happened to me. But there was a negative response, except from the secretary of the village hall committee, of which I was chairman, who wanted nothing to do with God but came as a favour to me.

After resisting for a long time, Olive committed her life to Christ and is still a pillar of the church. She was the first person to come to faith through my sharing my testimony.

Heaven alone knows how many more have been touched, but while there is breath in my body, I shall continue to share the good news of Jesus Christ, because I know that whoever lives without Jesus in their hearts misses out on the blessings through the blood covenant awaiting those who receive Him, and whoever dies outside of Christ faces an eternal destiny I would rather not think about.

I end this chapter with the testimony of Paul, the same Paul who was with me in Egypt. His testimony starts with suffering a serious back injury whilst serving in the Royal Marines at the age of seventeen. Over time this deteriorated until when he was thirty-four he started to suffer crippling pain. This continued for a period of six years before an operation improved the back's condition.

Then two years later the old symptoms began to reappear. It was then that Paul, now forty-two, received an invitation from a Christian friend to attend a dinner meeting of the Portsmouth chapter of the FGB. He accepted, he says, "partly for the free meal but also for the opportunity to 'take the mickey' out of his friend's Christianity", himself being a total cynic.

After the dinner, a speaker shared his story and then invited people up for prayer. Paul's friend encouraged Paul to go for prayer for his back. Paul refused the request twice, but then realised that if he did, he could go home.

As the speaker prayed Paul was hit by a terrific force, which knocked him off his feet backwards. When he stood up a little later, the speaker asked what he couldn't do before the prayer. Paul said that he hadn't touched his toes for eight years. When asked to do so by the speaker, he found he could now do so, without any pain. In fact, all the pain had left his body.

Paul couldn't sleep that night for fear that the pain would return, but it didn't, and hasn't, twenty-eight years later. In the meanwhile, Paul took up entering Ironman races, which involve swimming 3,800 metres, cycling 180 kilometres and running a full marathon – in under sixteen hours (in my opinion the nearest thing to madness). He has completed nine such races with all the training required, and never missed an opportunity to tell fellow competitors how he had been a cripple, and how Jesus had healed him.

That is the "full gospel" of Jesus Christ in action.

CHAPTER 19

The Power of God

> *"And now I will send the Holy Spirit, just as my Father promised. But stay here in the city until the Holy Spirit comes and fills you with power from heaven"* (Luke 24:49 NLT).
>
> *"John baptised with water, but in just a few days you will be baptised with the Holy Spirit"* (Acts 1:5 NLT).
>
> *"But you will receive **power** when the Holy Spirit comes upon you. And you will be my witnesses, telling people about me everywhere – in Jerusalem, throughout Judea, in Samaria and to the ends of the earth"* (Acts 1:8 NLT).

Before 1984 I never received within the church any teaching on the power of God, nor have I since. This led me, after my new birth, to seek training elsewhere. Both within FGB and outside on YouTube I learned that the power of God is what enables the gospel to spread and the church to grow, as was evidenced by the rapid spread of Christianity in the early years after Pentecost.

There are many ministries, some worldwide, streaming on YouTube showing staggering healings, in bodies and minds, as ministers pray in faith (that is under the anointing of the Holy Spirit with a sure expectation that the healing would result). And not only the ministers, because these ministries train their members to move in the power of the Holy Spirit leading to ever increasing congregations, who in turn go out and make more disciples.

I have always imagined that when the apostles and the disciples arrived for the first time in a town and started to tell of this man in Jerusalem who offered forgiveness of sins, had been crucified, had been raised by God from the dead, was alive and could heal people, and His name was Jesus, the hearers would have said words to the effect of, "Oh yeah? Prove it."

Surely the apostles would have seen someone in the crowd with some form of disability, perhaps a blind man, called him over, prayed for his healing in the name of Jesus, and he would be healed. Then all that man's friends would have asked how he was healed. Then they, too, would have heard about Jesus and people would start running to hear more, or, more likely, for their own healing, as they did when Jesus walked this earth and healed all that were sick, raised the dead and cast out demons. Paul would confirm that, I believe,

*"In mighty signs and wonders, by the **power** of the Spirit of God, so that from Jerusalem and round about to Illyricum I have fully preached the gospel of Christ"* (Romans 15:19).

As I have shared elsewhere, if *"Jesus is the same yesterday, today, and forever"* there is no reason why the church should not be operating in the same power today, if only it had the revelation of this fundamental truth of – and had the courage to move in – the power which God has made available to the church under the blood covenant.

The church must have had some revelation in 1978 of the power available to it, at least in the field of healing, when it passed the resolution on the role of healing in its ministry at the

Lambeth conference of that year, but which seems to have been filed and forgotten, (see chapter 22).

*"For God has not given us a spirit of fear, but of **power** and of love and of a sound mind"* (2 Timothy 1:7).

During a lifetime in the church, I can recall only one manifestation of the power of God moving in a service. On that occasion a friend of mine, John Wright, a member of FGB, came to the service and had a word of knowledge, which he shared, about someone having a pain in their neck. A lady came forward and was prayed for by my friend. Immediately, she said that the pain had gone. Later she said that she had suffered the pain for a long time and that the medication given to her by her doctor had not worked.

John was exercising one of the gifts of the Spirit set out in 1 Corinthians 12: the word of knowledge. The nine gifts of the Spirit were given to the universal church at Pentecost to equip the church to carry out its mission *"[making] disciples of all the nations, baptising them in the name of the Father and of the Son and of the Holy Spirit, teaching them to observe all things that I have commanded you; and lo, I am with you always, even to the end of the age"* (Matthew 28:19-20).

Yet I have, over the years, prayed, you might say "religiously", at the end of the communion service, "Send us out in the power of your Spirit to live and work to Your praise and glory." That sounds good, except without any teaching on the new birth and the baptism of the Holy Spirit, before 1984 I did not even understand that the Son and the Holy Spirit could come to live in me, let alone that *"He who is in you is greater than he who is in the world"* (1 John 4:4).

As it was, not yet being a Christian, I was going out without any understanding of who I could be in Christ or who He was in me, so, in effect, it was a meaningless prayer. All that changed for me in 1984 but, in my experience, the church remains silent on the dynamic power available to believers.

Having had the benefit of teaching from outside the church from men and women who teach on and move in the power of God, I now know that the "power" Jesus was talking about was and is the same power of the Holy Spirit that created the universe, as recorded in Genesis 1, and the very same power that raised Jesus from the dead. Paul prayed that:

*"The eyes of your understanding being enlightened; that you may know . . . what is the exceeding greatness of His **power** toward us who believe, according to the working of His mighty **power** which He worked in Christ when He raised Him from the dead and seated Him at His right hand in the heavenly places"* (Ephesians 1:18-20).

The same power is even closer to home when the word of God tells us:

"But if the Spirit of Him who raised Jesus from the dead dwells in you, He who raised Christ from the dead will also give life to your mortal bodies through His Spirit who dwells in you" (Romans 8:11).

*"Now to Him who is able to do exceedingly abundantly above all that we ask or think, according to the **power** which works in us, to Him be glory in the church by Jesus Christ to all generations"* (Ephesians 3:20-21).

Then, I also read among the many scriptures referring to the power of God:

"Most assuredly, I say to you, he who believes in Me, the works I do he will do also: and greater works than these he will do, because I go to My Father" (John 14:12).

As always, these spiritual truths would have seemed meaningless to my human mind (see chapter 5), but once I had been born again, baptised in the Holy Spirit and my spiritual eyes were opened, my understanding came to the point where I was able to move in that power (not my power but the power of the Holy Spirit moving through me in the name of Jesus), which I have done from time to time when led to do so.

I ask a question. Jesus walked this earth in His body preaching the kingdom of heaven, healing the sick, raising the dead, and casting out demons. These were signs that the kingdom of God was being manifest. After Jesus ascended into heaven, at Pentecost He created His body, the church, and empowered it to continue the works He had been doing, preaching the kingdom of heaven, healing the sick, raising the dead, and casting out demons in His name.

As explained in chapter 4, believers are by virtue of the blood covenant, through the new birth, recreated and empowered to be just like Him, and through the baptism of the Holy Spirit to have the same power as Jesus had. This was to be exercised through the power of attorney given to believers to act in His name. The book of the Acts of the Apostles records how they fulfilled that commission, so that the gospel spread widely, as recorded in that book. The preaching of the word was accompanied by signs and wonders as Jesus confirmed His word (Mark 16:20).

"And they went out and preached everywhere, the Lord working with them and confirming the word through the accompanying signs."

This last scripture alone asks the question: "if this was and is true, why is the church not manifesting the same dynamic mission today?"

CHAPTER 20

The Baptism in the Holy Spirit

"But you shall be baptised with the Holy Spirit not many days from now" (Acts 1:5).

This was yet another foundational teaching which was new to me. It is the empowering of believers for the ministry to which we are called. It is for some denominations controversial, and some even teach against it.

I have already shared when and how it happened to me as I was listening to the tape recording of the Guildhall meeting. Through it I became a different type of Christian from how I was before it occurred; not better but bolder immediately and becoming bolder still as I came to understand more about who I am in Christ.

This growth continues. I cannot recall ever trying to share my faith before, which is not surprising as I didn't have any real faith, but after that experience I had a boldness which became an embarrassment to friends and family as well as many in church. At the same time word went around among the local believers who had been baptised in the Holy Spirit and who were thrilled to hear of my conversion.

I got invited to meetings and soon was sharing my testimony of what had happened to me. It was that real!

It is surprising that there is so much opposition to the doctrine of the baptism of the Holy Spirit, as scripture seems unarguably clear about it. I refer to the following:

"I indeed baptise you with water; but One mightier than I is coming, whose sandal strap I am not worthy to loose. He will **baptise you with the Holy Spirit**" (Luke 3:16).

These words of John the Baptist are quoted in all four gospels.

"He commanded them not to depart from Jerusalem, but to wait for the Promise of the Father, 'which,' He said, 'you have heard from Me'" (Acts 1:4).

"But you shall receive power **when the Holy Spirit has come upon you**; and you shall be witnesses to Me in Jerusalem, and in all Judea and Samaria, and to the end of the earth" (Acts 1:8).

"For John truly baptised with water, but you shall **be baptised with the Holy Spirit** not many days from now" (Acts 1:5).

"Then I remembered the word of the Lord, how He said, 'John indeed baptised with water, but you shall **be baptised with the Holy Spirit**'" (Acts 11:16).

These scriptures have one thing in common; it is about the power of God, which was to come on them at Pentecost, with which the early church was endowed and is available to be exercised by the church today, if, as we read in Hebrews 13:8, "*Jesus Christ is the same yesterday, today, and forever.*"

There are three occasions in the New Testament where believers receiving the baptism of the Holy Spirit is recorded. In each case it is the outward evidence of speaking in tongues that distinguishes the receipt of the Spirit from all other occasions when the receipt of the gifts of the spirit was internal. The first time was at Pentecost, the second was in Acts chapters 10 and 19:

"*While Peter was still speaking these words, the* **Holy Spirit** *fell upon all those who heard the word. And those of the circumci-*

The Baptism in the Holy Spirit

*sion who believed were astonished, as many as came with Peter, because **the gift of the Holy Spirit** had been poured out on the Gentiles also. For they heard them speak tongues and magnify God"* (Acts 10:44-46).

*"When Paul had laid hands on them, **the Holy Spirit came upon them**, and they spoke with tongues and prophesied"* (Acts 19:6).

No doubt the controversy will continue, but in the meanwhile those who seek to live by *"every word that proceeds from the mouth of God"* will need to seek baptism in the Holy Spirit if they are to move in the power of the Holy Spirit, which, I trust, will become clearer from the scriptures which I have shared, and from my testimony and of others I have shared.

For further teaching on the baptism of the Holy Spirit, as well as on all aspects of our spiritual life, I recommend *The Spirit-Filled Believer's Handbook* by Derek Prince.[6]

"In his book Derek Prince explains that the preposition after "Baptism" in Greek can be translated either "in" or "with", which explains the variations of name. He prefers "in" as the most appropriate in the context of baptisms where the translation is "dunking".

---

[6] Derek Prince, *The Spirit Filled Believer's Handbook: Foundations for Christian Living from the Bible* (Milton Keynes: Nelson Word, 1994).

CHAPTER 21

The Name of Jesus

> *"Therefore God also has highly exalted Him and given Him **the name** which is above every name, that at **the name** of Jesus every name should bow"* (Philippians 2:9-10).

As soon as I joined the FGB I became aware that there was another dimension to the members of the chapter's faith in Jesus. It seemed to be that they knew somehow that the name of Jesus represented the power of God, and so, when used with faith in its power, the name of Jesus had the same power in the spiritual world, as well as in the physical world, that Jesus had exercised while on earth. Needless to say, evidence for this is found in the scriptures.

*"God has also highly exalted Him and given Him the **name** which is above every name, that at the **name** of Jesus every knee should bow, of those in heaven, and of those on earth, and of those under the earth, and that every tongue should confess that Jesus Christ is Lord, to the glory of God the Father"* (Philippians 2:9-11).

Even before Jesus had ascended to the Father His name had His authority.

*"Then the seventy returned with joy, saying, 'Lord, even the demons are subject to us in Your **name**"* (Luke 10:17).

Significantly, the seventy said the demons *"are subject to us **in** Your name".*

> "And Jesus came and spoke to them, saying, 'All authority has been given to Me in heaven and on earth. Go therefore and make disciples of all nations . . . teaching them to observe all things I have commanded you" (Matthew 28:18-20).

> "Let it be known to you all, and to all the people of Israel, that by the **name** of Jesus Christ of Nazareth, whom you crucified, whom God raised from the dead, by Him this man stands here before you whole" (Acts 4:10).

Teaching on the ministry of healing, and in particular the power in the name of Jesus, is for others who are called and anointed to do that. All I need say is that up to 1984 I knew nothing of it, and the relevant scriptures meant nothing to me.

Since then, the same scriptures became a part of my life. I have ministered healing, using the power of attorney which I have been given to minister in His name, seeing people touched by the Holy Spirit's power in this country and abroad.

Whoever is born again and baptised in the Holy Spirit needs to be ready to exercise this power for the extension of God's kingdom and for His glory, not to mention that it can lead to the salvation of souls, the healing of bodies and people being set free from whatever may be binding them.

But, at the start. it does mean stepping outside one's comfort zone. The first thought is, "What if it doesn't work?" That can trump the question, "What if it does work?" To begin with it takes courage but know that it is God whose reputation is at risk and, in my experience, He, recognising that we are on a learning curve, honours our boldness, and we are encouraged to do it again.

John Wimber, who had a major ministry in the 1990s, told of how for the first year of his seeking to minister healing, not one person he prayed for was healed, but he persisted. At the beginning of the next year thousands were healed and his teaching influenced individual believers worldwide to minister healing in the power of the name of Jesus Christ.

Jesus gives us clear instructions on praying in His name.

*"Most assuredly, I say to you, he who believes in Me, the works that I do he will do also; and greater works than these he will do, because I go to My Father. And whatever you ask in **My name**, that I will do, that the Father may be glorified in the Son. If you ask anything in **My name**, I will do it"* (John 14:12-14).

These directions of Jesus must be understood through spiritual eyes because when we speak them our words must be mixed with faith.

CHAPTER 22

Healing

"These signs will follow those who believe . . . they will lay hands on the sick, and they will recover" (Mark 16:17-18).

Some time ago I learned from a passing bishop that healing is a recognised part of the ministry of the church. He referred to a resolution at the Lambeth Conference of 1978. This is recorded as:

"The Conference praises God for the renewal of the ministry of healing within the Churches in recent times and reaffirms:

1. that the healing of the sick in his name is as much a part of the proclamation of the Kingdom as the preaching of the good news of Jesus Christ;
2. that to neglect this aspect of ministry is to diminish our part in Christ's total redemptive activity;
3. that the ministry to the sick should be an essential element in any revision of the liturgy."

I take that resolution as evidence that I should, together with every other member of the church, have received instruction on the importance of healing within the ministry of the church, and so be equipped to minister healing at the same time as sharing the gospel. Hebrews 6:1-2 tells me that the *"laying on of hands"* is one of the *"elementary principles of Christ"*. Should that not also be the attitude of every follower of Jesus?

I guess that when the bishops at that Lambeth Conference were considering the resolution they would have considered Exodus 15:26:

"If you diligently heed the voice of the Lord your God and do what is right in His sight, give ear to His commandments and keep all His statutes, I will put none of the diseases on you which I have brought on the Egyptians. For I am the Lord who heals you."

In the Old Testament God reveals aspects of His character through the names that He gives Himself. In that verse God discloses His name as "Jehovah Rapha" which means *"The Lord who heals you"*. If He no longer is the Lord who heals us, then He would have to change His name.

Until 1984 I was totally unaware of this key aspect of Christian ministry, but as soon as I joined the FGB I was introduced to it as a normal part of the Fellowship's vision, which was based on the statement that "if it is in the Bible, we believe it".

I also soon found YouTube recordings of ministries where men who have received an anointing for praying for the sick laid hands on the sick, or just spoke to the disease in Jesus' name, with awesome results. Unfortunately, as I have mentioned, I have heard of congregations being warned off such men if only on the grounds that some are very rich, and they have their own aircraft. The fact that they also have major worldwide ministries and bible colleges where thousands are brought to faith and discipled in the full gospel, is ignored.

As previously described, the FGB vision was of laymen witnessing through their testimonies, with the Lord confirming His word with signs and wonders as members prayed for healing in the lives of those the Lord led us to, following Jesus' instructions to His disciples which were to *"preach, saying, 'The* kingdom of heaven is at hand.' Heal the sick . . . raise the dead, cast out demons"* (Matthew 10:7-8).

My story concerning the healing ministry is simply that I was introduced to it as the norm for born-again Spirit-filled Christians, and since then over the years I have followed the scripture.

"And these signs will follow those who believe: In My name they will cast out demons; they will speak with new tongues; they will take up serpents . . . they will lay hands on the sick, and they will recover" (Mark 16:17-18).

I have assisted in the casting out of demons, I do speak in other tongues but have not taken up serpents. I have laid hands on the sick and they have recovered. To that extent the scripture is confirmed in my life's experience.

The last person I prayed for as at the time of writing this book was my grandson who had had a painful back for some time which interfered with his sport. He was and remains healed and is back playing rugby.

There are, of course, several "headline" scriptures telling us that God heals, for instance in the Old Testament, *"who forgives all your iniquities, who heals all your diseases"* (Psalm 103:3) and Isaiah 53:4-6 and in the New Testament, *"who Himself bore our sins in His own body on the tree, that we, having died to sins, might live for righteousness – by whose stripes you were healed"* (1 Peter 2:24).

"When evening had come, they brought to Him many who were demon-possessed. And He cast out the spirits with a word, and healed all who were sick, that it might be fulfilled which was spoken by Isaiah the prophet, saying: 'He Himself took our infirmities and bore our sicknesses'" (Matthew 8:16-17).

If the prophecy of healing was fulfilled by Jesus, it is surely fulfilled today if only we believe it and act on it. If we are not doing that then we are not only being disobedient to God's call on our lives but also robbing others of their healing, which Jesus won for them on the cross. After all, Jesus healed all who were sick, and He teaches us:

"Most assuredly, I say to you, he who believes in Me, the works that I do he will do also; and greater works than these he will do, because I go to My Father" (John 14:12).

It was through the blood covenant that healing for those born again into the kingdom of heaven was made available, to believers for themselves as well as ministering to unbelievers as evidence of the kingdom of heaven and leading people to Jesus.

"If I cast out demons with the finger of God, surely the kingdom of God has come upon you" (Luke 11:20).

So it is not just the sick believer who would be robbed but the unbeliever, because what was behind the swift spread of the gospel around the Mediterranean in the early years of the church were the "signs and wonders", which should be happening today, and is indeed happening in bible believing churches in the UK and is indeed happening in many countries in the developing world where the full gospel is being preached, drawing many into the kingdom.

CHAPTER 23

The Narrow Gate and The Broad Gate

> *"Strive to enter through the narrow gate, for many, I say to you, will seek to enter and will not be able"* (Luke 13:24).
>
> *"Enter by the narrow gate; for wide is the gate and broad is the way that leads to destruction, and there are many who go in by it. Because narrow is the gate and difficult is the way which leads to life, and there are few who find it"* (Matthew 7:13-14).

Here are two potentially scary verses on which I have never heard any teaching, yet they contain a warning from Jesus Himself which commands our attention. Here's one good reason.

One morning I was listening to teaching on Premier Christian Radio when the first words I heard, spoken by a pastor of a huge evangelical church, were, "There is no deception with more terrifying consequences than to believe you are a Christian when you are not. Surely that is the case for countless people."

Who can argue with that? Yet I, knowing what I know now, realise that if I had not sought the truth in 1984, I could still be heading for the broad gate and destruction. What a terrifying thought! And I would have been just one of those "countless people" if the pastor was correct.

Scripture itself makes it clear that people with a genuine but wrong belief can stumble at the critical moment. Take, for instance, the foolish bridesmaids in Mathew 25:12, or the wonder workers in Mathew 7:21.

It follows that everyone coming to Christ must be taught the condition precedent to our entry into the kingdom of heaven based on the inerrant truth of the word of God, which condition is dealt with unambiguously by Jesus in John 3:5 where He says to that very religious Pharisee Nicodemus, *"Most assuredly, I say to you, **unless** one is born of water and the Spirit, he cannot enter the kingdom of God."*

This is where the boast of the Church of England that it is a broad church becomes alarming, by virtue of this one verse in the Bible laying down the universal condition precedent for entry into the kingdom. No amount of reasoning or tradition can change that. Yet in all my many years in the church I have never received any teaching that I needed to be born again of water and the Spirit.

It must have been assumed that I and everyone else in the church were Christians. So, what I have shared of the wonderful transformation believers enjoy on our new birth – becoming a new creation with the past wiped out, being made the righteousness of God in Christ, access to the throne room, the brotherhood of Jesus, power over the works of the devil, healing, and so much more (see chapter 9) – never made the agenda.

I ask, how can the church be so silent about God's amazing provision? Once again, the words "daylight robbery" spring to mind, robbing not just believers but also those outside.

The church, the body of Christ, is no more than the sum of its members. Unless those members are discipled into the truth of scripture, born again, empowered by the same power which raised Jesus from the dead, and experiencing the truth of scripture, the world outside will never hear about, let alone experience, the wonder of the full gospel.

But if only the church were to move in signs and wonders which confirm the word, as the early church moved in them and grew exponentially through that witness, the same would happen here. If only!

John Wesley believed in terms that the evidence of the truth of scripture was found in it being experienced. I agree with that, which is one of the foundational pillars of this book. My story is the story of just one man who dares to believe in the truth of scripture and acts on that truth, and I trust that the evidence of that can be found in the story I tell.

The story unfolds as I read and absorbed God's handbook for life in Him, as I obeyed His commands, which led over time to my experiencing and moving, to the best of my ability, in the works which He had planned for me before the beginning of time. My hope and belief is that what I have shared will encourage others to step out of the box of the church's reasoning and traditions, and into the truths revealed in scripture.

For some, that may necessitate receiving the new birth by the Holy Spirit from above, and, as their spiritual eyes are opened, they are set free to receive that which, until then, they may have been robbed of, namely the exceedingly great and precious promises which the God they worship has provided for them through the blood covenant, and thereby the more abundant life – *"above all that we ask or think, according to the power that works in us"* (Ephesians 3:21).

This is our true inheritance, together with all other born-again believers while we remain on this earth, before going on to receive our *"crown of glory that does not fade away"* (1 Peter 5:4).

If, following the new birth, we continue in the word of God, we will come to know the truth and the truth will indeed set us free (John 8:32). Then the teaching on the two gates will not trouble us. Nor will we tremble when the books are opened on the day of judgement (Revelation 20:15).

Being a Christian is a serious business, much more serious than many of us may have been led to believe, if only because, *"Blessed are those who do His commandments, that they may have the right to the tree of life and may enter through the gates into the city"* (Revelation 22:14).

So the Bible ends as it started, with dire warning of the consequences of failure to follow our God's commandments. I see in that verse a clear indication of who may enter the narrow gate: likewise, by implication, who will not be welcome.

In present times an observer of the church might well believe, and he would be right, that obeying the commands of God coming down to us through His word is in fact, in the current spiritual climate, a cause of existential division. The newspaper headlines more than confirm that. Not only that but also that existential division is leading, according to polls, to the terminal decline of the church.

How has this come about? I would dare to suggest that an answer could well be the church's failure to teach and commit to belief in, and the working out in the daily life of the church, the instructions to the church – which is the Body of Christ – to do what He did; that is, doing only what He saw His Father doing and saying only what He heard His Father saying, in other words living by every word that proceeds from the mouth of God, which includes the words of scripture, preaching the kingdom of heaven, healing the sick, raising the dead and casting out demons.

In the case of Adam, it was the devil who deceived him, through Eve, that God's word could be doubted. The devil started by asking her, *"Did God really say you must not eat the fruit from any of the trees in the garden?"* (3:1 NLT).

In recent times some church leaders, and others within the church, seem to have been deceived into asking a similar question, but in a different context.

What is now being questioned is whether God's word, given and recorded during the period covered by the Bible, can be reinterpreted in the light of current social norms. Or, putting it in another way, "Did God really mean, *'His word endures for ever, and this is the word which by the gospel is preached unto you'?"* (See 1 Peter 1:25.)

This exercise of second-guessing God's commands opens the door for deception to creep in because there is no standard by which the proposed changes can be judged other than scriptures which are under challenge.

I, for one, have always understood that God's love is behind His commandments, which are given not just to lay down instructions for our behaviour but to protect us from becoming engaged in those things that are abhorrent to Him because they are not from above, which is the source of all good things (James 1:17), however good and reasonable they may seem according to the new social norms.

It must behove every believer who challenges the word of God to consider the Two Gates. One is wide and easy and leads to destruction; the other, the narrow one, is hard to enter but leads to life. Let him remember that *"Heaven and earth shall pass away, but My words will by no means pass away"* (Mathew 24:35).

We must be aware that at which gate we arrive will be governed by the decisions we have made during this life.

"Whoever has ears, let them hear what the Spirit says to the churches" (Revelation 2:29, 3:22 NLT).

CHAPTER 24

Hell

> "I was a stranger and you did not take Me in, naked and you did not clothe Me, sick and in prison and you did not visit Me . . . And these will go away into everlasting punishment" (Matthew 25:43, 46).

I don't recall ever hearing a sermon or any teaching on hell, yet what happens when we die is a question of eternal life or eternal death for every human being. Jesus, throughout His ministry, warned of the fate so many would experience when they fell short of the standards He demonstrated and taught us to follow. The parable of the sheep and goats is one example where the goats found themselves consigned to eternal punishment when they were unaware of any wrongdoing.

One of the many things that surprises me about my fellow men in, at least, the privileged social environment in which the Lord has placed me, is the seemingly total disinterest in what happens when we die. I once heard of the story of the maternity unit where there was a sign on the wall: "Don't forget that the first five minutes of a child's life are the most dangerous." A wag had written underneath, "The last five are pretty dodgy too!"

Effectively the devil, for whom together with his angels, Jesus tells us, hell was prepared (Matthew 25:41), with the willing help of man has reduced the existence of hell to a joke. "I would rather go to hell than heaven because heaven sounds so boring, and all my friends will be in hell," is something I have heard more than once.

But after 1984 when I started to take the Bible seriously, I was soon wondering about the truth of the reality of hell. My new Christian friends were able to tell me of books and websites recording testimonies of men and women to whom the Lord had revealed the horror of hell, some of which I have read or watched. Common to them is the instruction by Jesus to the person involved to warn the world of the fate of those who die outside Jesus.

The story of Bill Wiese in his book *23 Minutes in Hell*[7] is just one of many testimonies available online of men and women having experiences of hell. The book is not a comfortable read, but to be forewarned is to be forearmed.

I found on the web a 1996 report of the Church of England about "Hell" under the heading "Church of England Commission says Hell is the Same but Different"[8] which states:

> "A Church of England commission has rejected the idea of hell as a place of fire, pitchforks, and screams of unending agony, describing it instead as annihilation for all who reject the love of God . . . Rejecting the medieval vision of the underworld, the report said: 'Christians have professed appalling theologies which made God into a sadistic monster and left searing psychological scars on many' . . . There are many reasons for this change, but among them have been the moral protests from both within and without the Christian faith against a religion of fear, and a growing sense that the picture of a God who consigned millions

---

[7] soulchoiceministries.org
[8] apnews.com/article/611c8aa8904dde105806f6c05485f995

to eternal torment was far removed from the revelation of God's love in Christ.

Hell is not eternal torment, but it is the final and irrevocable choosing of that which is opposed to God so completely and so absolutely that the only end is total non-being."

There is no scriptural support for this statement that has resulted from unredeemed man's natural response to the idea of hell, which can certainly seem all those things that are laid against God when taken out of context.

But here again the gulf between those expressing those opinions and those born again and baptised in the Holy Spirit comes in to play. I say that because, as always, the spiritual truths of the bible need to be seen and understood through spiritual eyes. I can't imagine what eyes are needed to understand what "total non-being" or "annihilation" mean.

If I were instructed to defend God in court I would, in response to the charge that God is a sadistic monster, plead the love of the Father who sent His only and beloved Son to suffer the most excruciating death, to save all mankind, not one of whom deserves it, from the consequences of our sin.

"For God so loved the world that He gave His only begotten Son, that whoever believes in Him should not perish but have everlasting life" (John 3:16).

In so doing God gives each person a choice. On the one hand there is the free offer of eternal light, love, peace and happiness for those who choose it; on the other hand, if one chooses not, God gives you what you have chosen. *"The Lord has anointed Me to preach good tidings to the poor . . . to proclaim the acceptable year of the Lord, and the day of vengeance of our God"* (Isaiah 61:1-2).

I can't help thinking that those who challenge the character and words of God forget that He is their creator and our primary source about hell is Jesus.

The story of the potter and the marred clay in Jeremiah 18 underlines how just as the potter decides how he would mould the clay, so Israel in the Old Testament, and now us under the blood covenant, are, as if we need to be told it, in no position to dictate to God, our creator.

I should also mention that I, along with every other member of the Church of England, acknowledge in saying the Apostles' Creed, that Jesus was "crucified, died, and was buried; He descended into hell. On the third day He rose again . . ." We are not told where Jesus spent those three days and nights if hell does not exist.

And to avoid any doubt, Article of Religion VIII confirms the three creeds which "ought thoroughly to be received and believed: for they may be proved by most certain warrants of Holy Scripture".

"Members of the Jury, the evidence is clear. It is not God who sends people to hell. They go because of their own choice."

I rest my case!

CHAPTER 25

The Devil

"Your adversary the devil walks about like a roaring lion, seeking whom he may devour" (1 Peter 5:8).

To be forewarned is to be forearmed. It is therefore necessary for every believer to know who is his or her adversary.

One of the many consequences of putting one's faith in *"every word that proceeds from the mouth of God"* is the understanding that the devil is real, and that from the time of the fall of Adam in Genesis he has been at war with God in the Old Testament and with Christians in the New Testament. He is alive and active in his mission.

His mission is *"to steal, and to kill, and to destroy"* (John 10:10). If he can steal the word of God from the believer, then he has succeeded in his mission because death and destruction will be the fate of the then unbeliever.

We also need to know the limitation on his power. He lost this in his battle with Jesus when Jesus descended to hell after his crucifixion and took back the keys. He is now powerless, and his only modus operandi is using deception, just as he did in the Garden of Eden. Jesus said of him, *"He was a murderer from the beginning, and does not stand in the truth, because there is no truth in him. When he speaks a lie, he speaks from his own resources, for he is a liar and the father of it"* (John 8:44).

I have never heard any teaching on the devil, so I was never forewarned to be forearmed. The devil rarely, or at all, got a mention. Yet in Ephesians 6:10-13 I read that he is a genuine and real threat to me.

"Finally, my brethren, be strong in the Lord and in the power of His might. Put on the whole armour of God, that you may be able to stand against the wiles of the devil. For we do not wrestle against flesh and blood, but against principalities, against powers, against the rulers of the darkness of this age, against the spiritual hosts of wickedness in the heavenly places. Therefore take up the whole armour of God, that you may be able to withstand in the evil day, and having done all, to stand."

The devil's main tool is to sow fear in the believer, to counter his faith. Non-believers are, of course, no threat to him unless they are moving towards faith in Jesus.

Because I did not even know he existed, I had no awareness of the threat he is to Christians, nor of our authority over him, nor of my need of it.

He was more of a joke about a mythical figure. I heard read regularly in my BC days at our son's prep school's evensong, *"Your adversary the devil walks about like a roaring lion, seeking whom he may devour"* (1 Peter 5:8), which we joked about on the way home as it seemed so inappropriate for young boys to hear every week! Note, the devil is not a roaring lion, he is just pretending to be one.

Then in the first letter of John I read a statement which surprised and shocked me. I hear so often that God is in control of everything that happens on earth, and so gets blamed for allowing it. But what John writes in the following verse paints a very different picture.

The Devil

"We know that we are children of God and that the world around us is under the control of the evil one" (1 John 5:19 NLT).

Yes, God, the creator of the heavens and the earth, is indeed in ultimate control but, as explained earlier in the book, He had surrendered all His authority over the earth to Adam before the fall which in turn was surrendered to the devil, who has been operating unopposed in the earth until Jesus, who, having defeated him in hell, is reclaiming God's earth and its inhabitants through men and women (us) who have been *"delivered... from the power of darkness and conveyed... into the kingdom of the Son of His love"* (Colossians 1:13).

"For this purpose, the Son of God was manifested, that He might destroy the works of the devil" (1 John 3:8).

"You are of God, little children, and have overcome them, because He who is in you is greater than he who is in the world" (1 John 4:4).

If we know our enemy and how to use the armour as well as our authority over him, we need not fear the devil. Have I experienced attacks from our enemy? I most certainly have. Have I won the battle on every occasion? Again, I most certainly have, but not always without a struggle.

The default response is, *"God resists the proud but gives grace to the humble. Therefore submit to God. Resist the devil and he will flee from you"* (James 4:6-7).

I have learned that the most effective way of attack and defence is to adopt Jesus' strategy, which was to quote the word of God: *"It is written..."* (Luke 4:8,10). The devil had no defence to that because he is a defeated foe.

Jesus clearly wants us to know of the threat that the devil can be to Christians because in John 17:15 He prays to the Father, *"I do not pray that You should take them out of the world, but that You should keep them from the evil one." when* we too play our part when we pray in the Lord's prayer *"Deliver us from evil"* or, in many translations, *"deliver us from the evil one"*

I repeat, "to be forewarned is to be forearmed". To be forewarned by Jesus, puts us in a winning position if only we listen to Him.

CHAPTER 26

"The Conclusion of the Whole Matter"

> "Let us hear the conclusion of the whole matter: Fear God and keep His commandments, for this is man's all" (Ecclesiastes 12:13).

God does not change, *"I am the Lord, and I do not change"* (Malachi 3:6 NLT), and His word endures for ever, *"But the word of the Lord endures for ever"* (1 Peter 1:25).

Solomon's conclusion is another way of saying that, *"man shall not live by bread alone; but man lives by every word that proceeds from the mouth of the Lord"* (Deuteronomy 8:3), which Jesus quoted to the devil, who had to withdraw, being unable to challenge it. There is power in the word of God.

This book is not about me. It is about the truth of the word of God. *"What is truth?"* Pilate asked Jesus in response to Jesus saying to him, *"For this cause I was born, and for this cause I have come into the world, that I should bear witness to the truth. Everyone who is of the truth hears My voice"* (John 18:37-38).

In the previous chapter Jesus prayed for His disciples.

"They are not of the world, just as I am not of the world. Sanctify them by Your truth. Your word is truth. As you sent Me into the world, I also have sent them into the world. And for their sakes I sanctify Myself, that they also may be sanctified by the truth" (John 17:16-19).

I see two main factual statements emerging from these scriptures. First, the most obvious one, which is that Jesus, according to the word, is truth personified. It follows that if truth is a person, then it ceases to be relative. It leaves no room for believers to make up their own minds.

Secondly, that the truth, when believed, has a sanctifying effect on the believer. Sanctification is defined commonly as "being set apart for God's special use and purpose".

So, I dare to believe that my acceptance of the word of God as revealing all truth sanctified me and continues to do so.

That is, it set me apart for God's special use and purpose, which becomes the fulfilment of the prophetic word in 1984, "I see you walking across a plain saying, 'Thus says the Lord.'" This privilege of being set apart for God's special use and purpose is available to whosoever comes to faith, is born again, and through eyes of faith receives revelation of the inerrancy of the scriptures and walks in the truth of them.

I trust that the pieces of the puzzle by now are coming together in some form or shape, revealing, if only through a glass darkly, an overall picture of what God has given us through the blood covenant and the exceedingly great and precious promises, so that we not only may enjoy the abundant life which Jesus says to His sheep He came to give us – *"I have come that they may have life, and that they may have it more abundantly"* (John 10:10) – but also be equipped to be His ambassadors in sharing the good news of the gospel to a dark and hurting world.

What I have shared, albeit in a light and non-exhaustive, even simplistic way (some might say), for I have taken the scriptures at their plain meaning, are some foundational truths which make up the picture. By quoting scriptures I am effectively saying, "Thus says the Lord."

I set out from the time of my churchyard encounter in 1984 to find out whether God was even real! As recounted, He soon manifested His reality in powerful ways, which led me to go on to seek the answer to the further question, "Who am I in Christ?" because at an early stage I was beginning to realise that there was more to that than the church was telling me.

So, what do the scriptures reveal as to who I am in Christ, when seen through spiritual eyes, because the scriptures are referring to who my reborn, new creation, inner man is? *"For you died, and your life is hidden with Christ in God. When Christ who is our life appears, then you also will appear with Him in glory"* (Colossians 3:3-4). The scriptures reveal that:

I AM COMPLETE IN HIM

"For in Him dwells all the fullness of the Godhead bodily; and you are complete in Him, who is the head of all principality and power" (Colossians 2:9-10).

I AM LIKE JESUS

"Love has been perfected among us in this: that we may have boldness in the day of judgement; because as He is, so are we in this world" (1 John 4:17).

I AM FAULTLESS

"Now to Him who is able to keep you from stumbling, and to present you faultless before the presence of His glory with exceeding joy, to God our Saviour, who alone is wise, be glory and majesty, dominion and power, both now and forever. Amen" (Jude 1:24-25).

I AM FREE

"Then Jesus said to those Jews who believed in Him, 'If you abide in My word, you are My disciples indeed. And you shall know the truth, and the truth shall make you free'" (John 8:31-32).

In the opening of chapter 7, I share how when I discovered the exceedingly great and precious promises, I found the "purpose of my life and my destiny". It was to become "a partaker of the divine nature". It is also the destiny of every born-again believer, because in Ephesian 5:25-27 we read:

"Husbands, love your wives, just as Christ also loved the church and gave Himself for her, that He might sanctify and cleanse her with the washing of water by the word, that He might present her to Himself a glorious church, not having spot or wrinkle or any such thing, but that she should be holy and without blemish."

The story I have shared is an account of the trail I followed from staging post to staging post, where the fundamental truths were revealed; fundamental truths which every believer needs to visit and mark, learn, and inwardly digest and receive by faith the riches of each promise to arrive at our destination.

Before setting out it is necessary to be able to read the map. As we are about to travel into a spiritual kingdom where the word of God is our "satnav" we first need to have taken the following steps: repentance towards God, faith in Jesus Christ, and baptism in water and the Holy Spirit because flesh and blood cannot enter the kingdom of God. Thereby we will be truly reborn and will have eyes of faith through which the spiritual directions can be followed.

If, as Jesus said, we continue in the word, we will, as members of His church, experience His sanctifying and cleansing

"The Conclusion of the Whole Matter"

with the washing of water by the word. So we will know truly who we have been made to be in Christ: faultless, complete in Him, like Jesus and free, being partakers of the divine nature, and, as members of His church, His bride, free from *"spot or wrinkle or any such thing"* but *"holy and without blemish"*, and, of course, *"the righteousness of God in Christ"*.

If that sounds to the reader that I am claiming to be perfect, I need to point out that what God has made me to be in my inner, reborn, spirit man and what I am as at today is not the same. My part is to seek by faith to grow spiritually to become more and more like Him and so to reflect in my life the attributes I have listed in the previous paragraphs.

Solomon (Ecclesiastes 12:13) and Moses (Deuteronomy 8:3) were right! Neither of them is just stating a fact, but revealing a living and active spiritual truth which is that this is the only way of life acceptable to God. That's our part; He will do the rest. He has covenanted to do so.

"Oh, the depth of the riches both of the wisdom and knowledge of God! How unsearchable are His judgments and His ways past finding out!" (Romans 11:33)

CHAPTER 27

Postscript: Facing the Challenge

> *"And they went out and preached everywhere, the Lord working with them and confirming the word through the accompanying signs"* (Mark 16:20).

I have mentioned, almost in passing, that seeking to live by every word that proceeds from the mouth of God has its challenges. No more so than when we have a health problem. This is the story of what happened when I was faced with just such a challenge, and how the Lord confirmed His word, as revealed through this book, by a spectacular sign.

In early June 2022 I discovered that there was a blockage in my bowel, which resulted in my total inability to pass anything solid or otherwise.

It is perhaps hard to exaggerate the seriousness of this, not only from a health perspective, but how I was to respond. The challenge was: should I respond as the world would naturally and urgently respond, by going straight to and relying on the doctor, accepting all the unpleasant things the medical profession would do to investigate and attempt to resolve it, or should I trust the word of God?

"Who Himself bore our sins in His body on the tree, that we, having died to sins, might live for righteousness – by whose stripes you were healed" (1 Peter 2:24).

If I took the doctor route, I would effectively be putting my life in the hands of, and so trusting, the medical profession. Yet I was at the time writing this book in which I was declaring not only that I was seeking *"to live by every word that proceeds from the mouth of God"* but was encouraging readers of the book to do likewise, because this is the command of God Himself to not just me but to every believer. If I went to the doctor, I would be disobedient to God's commandment and effectively deny the truthfulness of His word. This would mean that I would have to scrap the book.

I had also to face the possibility that things might not work out in the way I was relying on, which could in the worst scenario lead to my early death.

And then, what about telling Mary and the family, for who's sake I owed a duty of looking after myself, and who would never understand my not taking medical advice?

I agonised over this. I prayed about it but received no special direction from God, which, in retrospect, was to be expected because there is no point in asking God whether we should be obedient to His word. It was my decision.

What I did was to go back to what I have written in chapter 6 on faith, in which I have stressed that faith without works (or corresponding action) is dead.

"Thus also faith by itself, if it does not have works, is dead" (James 2:17).

In this context a "corresponding action" was necessary. There was only one such action which I could take if I was relying on the word of God, which said I was already healed by Jesus on the cross (see also chapter 22). It was to eat as normally as I would be doing if I was healed.

Postscript: Facing the Challenge

So, I resolved to eat normally, which would mean that Mary had no idea of my problem. From the beginning I continued to eat breakfast, lunch, and an evening meal, which Mary cooked every day. That was daily a not insubstantial amount of food.

The total blockage continued for at least two months, with gradual improvement thereafter continuing up to the publication of this book, when something tells me that there is absolutely no blockage.

During all this time, over the two months and thereafter, I ate normally and passed nothing. I had no symptoms of constipation or any discomfort, nor have I had any since. Throughout I ate well, felt well, and lived a normal life in every other way. No one would have had any inkling that I had a health problem.

If asked where the food went, I can only respond that God alone knows! I shared my miracle with Mary in early September when working parts were beginning to operate more normally.

I can only believe that this miraculous recreation of my digestive system was God's way of confirming His involvement in the book, to the point of ensuring that I did not bin it but was fit to finish it with confidence that it was His book and not mine. And, perhaps, He acted to confirm at my time of great need that He watches over His word to ensure that it achieves the purpose for which it is sent, as He promises, *"God is not a man, that He should lie, nor a son of man, that He should repent. Has He said, and will He not do? Or has He spoken, and will He not make it good?"* (Numbers 23:19).

That is my story (so far). I pray that the scriptures which I have quoted and my simple account of those scriptures becoming my experience will, through the Holy Spirit, reveal the power of the full gospel to transform the lives of believers, so they become equipped for service of the Master here and now, and go from being discipled to making disciples for the glory of God and the revival of His body, the church.

Acknowledgements

In coming to an understanding of the scriptures, I have, as indicated, resorted to many ministries through books, CDs, DVDs, YouTube recordings and daily broadcasts. I want to acknowledge my gratitude to them and at the same time, perhaps, encourage seekers to explore them in their search for the truth of the full gospel.

All these ministries' teachings are based on the inerrancy of scripture. They are not the only ministries I have followed, but the ones I continue to follow. I must also acknowledge my indebtedness to the Full Gospel Business Men's Fellowship International for my initiation into the world where the "Full Gospel" is manifest not only in word but in deed, and for training me to be a witness and to move in the power of God.

The principal ministries are:

E.W. Kenyon, who died in 1948 but whose ministry still flourishes worldwide today.

The Blood Covenant
In His Presence
Christ the Healer

And many more books which are available on Amazon and teaching on YouTube

Kenneth Copeland Ministries, a worldwide ministry whose stated mission is "to minister the Word of Faith by teaching believers who they are in Christ Jesus, taking them from the milk of the Word to the meat, and from religion to reality".

www.kcm.org

Andrew Wommack Ministries International, a worldwide ministry with powerful teaching and training on all aspects of Christian living.

www.awmi.net

Printed in Great Britain
by Amazon